NATIONAL
GEOGRAPHIC
KiDS

ESPN

IT'S A NUMBERS GAME!

FOOTBALL

The math behind the perfect punt, the game-changing interception, and so much more!

Eric Zweig

Foreword by NFL SUPERSTAR PATRICK MAHOMES

NATIONAL GEOGRAPHIC
WASHINGTON, D.C.

TABLE OF CONTENTS

The statistical data in this book are through the 2020 seasons, unless otherwise noted.

I think about time a lot when I'm on the football field. I make sure that I call a play before the play clock expires. My offensive linemen block the opposing team to give me enough time to make a play. Wide receivers, running backs, and tight ends run short and long plays. My teammates, coaches, and I use time, numbers, and math to help us win football games.

Play by play, quarter by quarter, game by game. When you think about those periods of time and what you can do to make the most of every second, amazing things can happen.

Imagine, it's the fourth quarter of Super Bowl LIV and my team, the Kansas City Chiefs, is down by 10 points with 8:53 left on the game clock. I know I need to choose plays that manage the clock so we can score more points before the clock hits zero. We run 10 plays in two minutes and 36 seconds and—boom—touchdown. 49ers: 20, Chiefs: 17. It's our time!

The Chiefs defense shuts down the opposing offense in three plays that take up one minute and three seconds of the remaining time on the game clock.

I get the ball back with 5:10 on the game clock. In seven plays and only two minutes and 20 seconds—touchdown! Chiefs: 24, 49ers: 20. Back on top!

The Chiefs defense gets the ball back in my hands with 1:25 on the game clock. Just two plays and five seconds later—touchdown. Chiefs: 31, 49ers: 20.

After a 49ers interception, we are in victory formation. As the last five seconds tick off the game clock, I throw a long and high pass deep right, watching the clock strike zero. We're Super Bowl Champs!

Of course, there are a lot more numbers in football besides the time remaining on the clock, but numbers help tell the story. Math is in every play, from calculating the down and distance of a drive, to adding up how many yards I need to throw a complete pass to a receiver, to the angle that the receiver cuts in a pass pattern to catch it. And every play adds more numbers to an athlete's statistics. Defensive players tally up their number of tackles, and kickers try their best to kick the longest kick they've ever made through the goal posts.

All of these numbers can be a lot to keep track of over the course of four quarters. Whether you want to learn how to tally your favorite player's statistics or call plays for your next flag football game, *It's a Numbers Game! Football* is for you. You'll learn about the math behind the game and read about some of the greatest players in football history. We'll help you calculate statistics, add up your fantasy football team points, and of course we've got all the numbers on the biggest game of the year—the Super Bowl.

Once you're ready to dig in to more football numbers, check out the activity at the end of chapter six. As part of the Read for 15 program from 15 and the Mahomies, I want you to start your own sports podcast or talk show with your friends! Choose your favorite football players to read about, and record yourself telling your friends what you learned. Maybe you'll decide to read about me and my stats!

So grab your calculator and a football and get ready to crunch some numbers because we're about to kick off!

#15

Patrick Mahomes

PATRICK MAHOMES GETS READY TO THROW A PASS DURING A GAME AGAINST THE BALTIMORE RAVENS IN 2019.

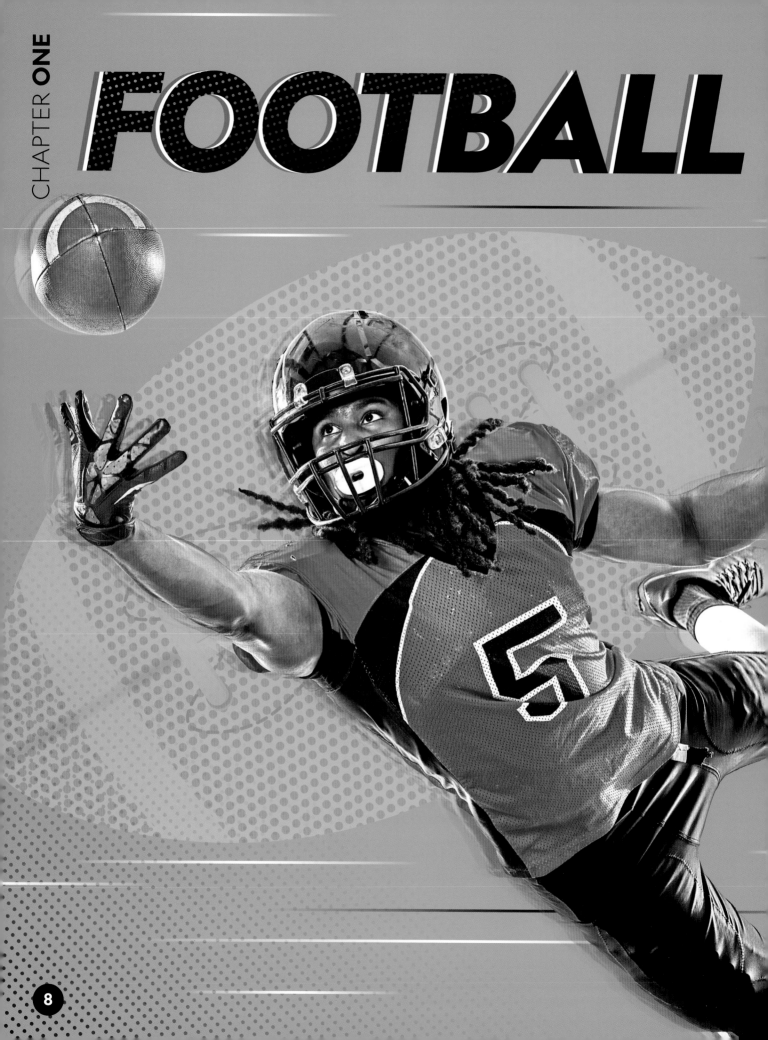

FOOTBALL

THROUGH THE YEARS

Numbers are everywhere in football. Some are easy to see if you watch the game—they are marked on the field every 10 yards, they glow on the scoreboard, and they are displayed on each player's uniform. Of course, there are also key statistical numbers accompanying nearly every play, too. People have been adding up all these numbers for more than 150 years. The game today is very different from the way it was when it got started. Here's a numbers-packed look at how football has grown and changed over the years.

DIGIT-YOU-KNOW?

In this book, we'll focus on football as it's played in the United States and Canada in the NFL and CFL. But football is more than just a professional sport. Here's a quick breakdown of football teams and leagues:

National Football League (NFL)	32 teams
Canadian Football League (CFL)	9 teams
U.S. college football	900* teams
Canadian universities	27 teams
U.S. high schools	16,000* teams
Canadian high schools	1,200* teams
U.S. youth league (Pop Warner) football	5,000* teams

*approximate number

WHEN *FOOTBALL BEGAN*

How long have people been playing football? The first official game in the United States was on November 6, 1869. On that day, Rutgers College beat what is now Princeton University 6–4. But what they played that fall day didn't look much like the football that we have now. So, how did the game come to be what it is today?

SOCCER + RUGBY = FOOTBALL

The first football games in the United States were based mainly on soccer. They were played with a round, soccerlike ball, and no one was allowed to throw the ball or pick it up and run with it. And, unlike today, there were 25 players on the field for each team. Having more players was similar to rugby, a game that students at Canadian universities played in the 1860s and 1870s.

Like soccer, rugby came from England. But rugby uses an oval ball, and the rules allow players to pick it up and run with it. In May 1874, the team from McGill University in Montreal, Canada, traveled to Massachusetts, U.S.A., to play a two-game series against Harvard University. Harvard players and their fans liked McGill's rugby rules much better than their own soccer-style game. They introduced rugby to other American universities, and the game caught on.

Still, there were some parts of the soccer-style game that players wanted to keep. Soon, teams began taking some of the things they liked from soccer and adding them to rugby. Then, in 1876, representatives from Rutgers, Yale, Princeton, and Columbia met to discuss the game. They came up with the first set of rules—lots more would come—for a brand-new type of football.

UNIVERSITY OF MICHIGAN PLAYERS

HISTORY BY THE NUMBERS

In 1880, soon after Americans started coming up with their own rules for football, the number of players on the field was reduced to 11. With fewer people on the field, players had more space to move around. This allowed the game to emphasize speed over strength as compared to rugby.

Today, the rules for youth and high school football allow for the game to be played with as few as nine, eight, or even six players on the field. Still, the standard for American football remains 11 players.

HIGH SCHOOL FOOTBALL ACTION IN SAN FRANCISCO, CALIFORNIA, IN 1937

DIGIT-YOU-KNOW?

In Canada, football stayed closer to its rugby roots longer than it did in the United States. Canada didn't reduce the number of players from the standard rugby lineup of 15 until 1903. Some leagues in Canada cut down to 12 players that year. None ever went down to 11. The standard in Canadian football remains 12 players to this day.

FOOTBALL *TODAY*

Football is America's game. The numbers prove it. On fall Friday nights, thousands of fans fill the seats at high school games all across the United States. On fall Saturdays, tens of thousands pack college stadiums from coast to coast. On Sundays, even more fans pour into stadiums for National Football League (NFL) games. Millions more watch games on TV at home. The NFL is the highest level of football a player can reach, and it's one of the most popular leagues for a spectator sport in the world.

KANSAS CITY CHIEFS VERSUS MIAMI DOLPHINS

GOING PRO

In the 1880s in the United States, football was played mainly by students at colleges and universities. After these players graduated, many of them still wanted a way to hit the field. So, they formed their own teams. As more fans came to watch their games, the rivalries between teams grew more intense. By the 1890s, teams began paying their top players. By the 1900s, a few U.S. states had enough teams to form professional leagues.

The NFL celebrated its 100th season during the fall and winter of 2019–2020. Before the NFL's first season in 1920, players used to jump from team to team and from league to league, and there wasn't always enough money to pay them. Forming one big league, where all the teams played by the same rules, seemed like the solution. Originally, this league was known as the American Professional Football Association. It didn't become the National Football League until 1922.

BUFFALO BILLS VERSUS NEW ENGLAND PATRIOTS

PENCIL POWER

Today, the NFL has two different conferences: the National Football Conference (NFC) and the American Football Conference (AFC). Each conference has four divisions: North, South, East, and West. Each of those divisions has four teams in them. Knowing all this, can you calculate how many teams there are in the NFL? For each conference, you'll have to multiply the number of teams in each division by the number of divisions there are, and then add up the two totals.

There are 32 teams in the NFL.

ANSWER: $(4 \times 4) + (4 \times 4) = 32$

THE INDIANAPOLIS COLTS AT SUPER BOWL XLI IN 2007

ROSTER SIZE

In the NFL, each team is permitted to have 53 players on its roster for every game, even though only 11 players can be on the field at a time. In the Canadian Football League, each team can have 12 players on the field, but they can only have 45 players on their roster. College football teams in the NCAA (National Collegiate Athletic Association) currently have a maximum of 125 players allowed on their rosters.

HISTORY BY THE NUMBERS

There were 14 teams in the NFL when the league began. The number of teams has jumped around a lot over the years. The biggest growth came in 1970 when the NFL officially merged with a rival league called the American Football League. Here's a look at how the numbers have gone up and down:

YEARS	TEAMS
1920	14
1930	11
1940	10
1950	13
1960	13
1970	26
1980	28
1990	28
2000	31
2002 to present	32

CHICAGO BEARS IN THE 1920S

CHICAGO BEARS IN 2014

DETROIT LIONS IN 1970

BASIC RULES: MOVING THE BALL

Football can be a complicated game. There's a lot going on out there on the field. So many rules, so many different plays. What's a fair catch? How many points was that score worth?

Sure, football can seem puzzling, but the basic idea is pretty simple. The offense—the team with the ball—tries to move the ball down the field and into the other team's end zone, or the area beyond the goal line at the end of the field, for a touchdown. To move the ball, a player can run with it until he is stopped. Or a player can throw it downfield to a teammate. The team without the ball—the defense—tries to stop the offense from advancing. Mostly, they do this by attempting to tackle the ballcarrier. In football, tackling means to grab hold of someone and try to knock them down.

To keep possession of the ball, the offensive team needs to gain at least 10 yards in four plays (known as downs). When a team has moved the ball 10 yards or more—whether that takes them one down, two downs, three downs, or four—a first down is earned, and the team gets four more downs to try to advance 10 yards again. A touchdown (see page 16) can be scored on a play from anywhere on the field and on any down. If the defense stops the offense before it gains 10 yards, its team takes over the ball and gets to go on offense. In Canadian football, teams only get three downs to make 10 yards.

WASHINGTON WIDE RECEIVER JEFF BADET CAN'T MAKE A CATCH AGAINST DETROIT.

PENCIL POWER

The Tennessee Titans have the ball against the Jacksonville Jaguars. On first down, Titan quarterback Ryan Tannehill hands the ball to star running back Derrick Henry. He gains eight yards before being tackled. On second down, Tannehill hands off to Henry again, who goes straight up the middle. This time, the Jacksonville defense pushes him back for a two-yard loss. On third down, Tannehill fires a short pass up the middle to wide receiver Julio Jones. It's a gain of six yards.

Has Tennessee gained enough yards on these three plays to make a first down? Add or subtract the yards gained or lost on each play to see if the total comes to more than 10 yards.

ANSWER: 8 − 2 + 6 = 12.
Tennessee has gained 12 yards, so the Titans have earned a first down.

RYAN TANNEHILL

SCRIMMAGE AND DOWNS

Every offensive play in football begins with the ball placed on the field and the two teams in formation facing each other along the line of scrimmage, the starting line for the play. The line of scrimmage is actually just an imaginary line—although TV broadcasts usually display it with graphics. Neither team is allowed to move across the line until the play on each new down has started. Every down begins with a player known as the center snapping the ball (throwing it backward between his legs) directly to another player on his team (usually the quarterback) behind him.

When the line of scrimmage was introduced to football in 1880, there was no rule about getting a first down. Some teams would hog the ball and take their time by only moving the ball a yard or two on each down.

So, a new rule was passed in 1882. Teams would have to move the ball at least five yards on three downs or else the other team would get it. The rule was eventually changed in 1912 to give teams four downs, instead of only three, to get 10 yards. Canadian football never added a fourth down. Three downs to make 10 yards remains the rule in Canadian football to this day.

THE CHICAGO BEARS AND THE NEW ORLEANS SAINTS AT THE LINE OF SCRIMMAGE

BASIC RULES: *SCORING POINTS*

So, your team has earned a first down. That's good ... but it's just a step in the right direction. To win a football game, you have to score the most points. These are the four ways you can score points. The point totals are the same in the NFL, the CFL, and the NCAA.

TOUCHDOWN

A touchdown is scored when a player carries the ball across the opponent's goal line and into the end zone or catches the ball inside the end zone. How many points is a touchdown worth? Six points? Seven? Eight? The answer is ... all of the above! A touchdown earns a team six points, but as soon as that play is complete, the team has the chance to score more points on another play. Depending on the results, they can gain one extra point for a total of seven or two points for a total of eight.

STEFON DIGGS OF THE BUFFALO BILLS CATCHES A TOUCHDOWN PASS.

TRY AFTER TOUCHDOWN

There are two ways for a team to try for extra points after a touchdown. One way is by lining up a specified distance from the defensive team's goal line and kicking the ball through the goal posts. (The distance is 15 yards in the NFL, 25 yards in the CFL, and three yards in college and high school football.) If the kick is successful, the team scores one extra point. This is usually referred to as the "point after," the "extra point," a "conversion" (American football), a "convert" (Canadian football), or a "PAT" (point after touchdown). In the NFL, a team can try to score two extra points after a touchdown by lining up two yards from the defensive team's goal line (or three yards in the CFL and college football) and either running the ball or completing a pass into the end zone. This is called a "two-point conversion" or a "two-point convert."

BEN GROGAN OF OKLAHOMA STATE KICKS A PAT.

FIELD GOAL

A field goal is when a team kicks the ball up and through the goal posts at the back of the other team's end zone. (Goal posts are on the goal line in Canadian football.) The ball must be kicked from a spot on the ground on or behind the line of scrimmage. Once the ball is kicked, it must not touch the ground or any other offensive player before it goes through the goal posts. A field goal is worth three points.

SAFETY

A safety is when the defensive team stops the other team's offense behind its own goal line inside its own end zone. It doesn't happen very often in a football game, but when it does the defensive team earns two points for a safety.

DIGIT-YOU-KNOW?

Kicking for one point after a touchdown is successful more than 90 percent of the time, while trying for two points only works about 50 percent of the time.

PENCIL POWER

The 2013 Denver Broncos set an NFL record for touchdowns in one season with 76. Their kicker, Matt Prater, successfully added 75 extra points and also booted 25 field goals. The total points scored by the Broncos that season also set an NFL record. To figure out how many points Denver scored overall, use this formula for points earned in touchdowns, extra points, two-point conversions, and field goals.

Remember: Touchdown = 6 points, Extra point = 1 point, Field goal = 3 points

Here's the formula:

$$+ \begin{array}{l} \textbf{(Touchdowns} \times \textbf{6)} \\ \textbf{(Extra points} \times \textbf{1)} \\ \textbf{(Field goals} \times \textbf{3)} \\ \hline \textbf{Total points scored} \end{array}$$

ANSWER: (76 × 6) + (75 × 1) + (25 × 3), which is: 456 + 75 + 75 = 606 total points scored.

DENVER BRONCOS KICKER
MATT PRATER

TIME TO *PLAY!*

Traditionally, in the game's early days, fall was football season. Today, the NFL plays its regular season from September until December with playoffs in January leading up to the Super Bowl in February. College football in the NCAA often begins in late August and wraps up with bowl games and a championship game in December and January. In Canada, the CFL season begins in June and ends with the playoffs in November. During these football-filled months, fans and players are always watching the giant stadium clock ticking down the seconds. From the first month of the season to the last second on the clock, time matters in football.

ON THE SCHEDULE

How many games does each NFL team play during the regular season? Let's find out.

Since the league grew to 32 teams in 2002, there have been four key points the NFL uses each year in its scheduling formula:

EVERY TEAM PLAYS:

• One home game and one road game against its three division opponents

$$
\begin{array}{r} 2 \\ \times\ 3 \\ \hline 6\ \text{games} \end{array}
$$

• One game against all four teams in another division in its own conference

$$
\begin{array}{r} 1 \\ \times\ 4 \\ \hline 4\ \text{games} \end{array}
$$

• One game against one team each from the two other divisions in its own conference

$$
\begin{array}{r} 1 \\ \times\ 2 \\ \hline 2\ \text{games} \end{array}
$$

• One game against all four teams in another division in the other conference

$$
\begin{array}{r} 1 \\ \times\ 4 \\ \hline 4\ \text{games} \end{array}
$$

• Starting in 2021, every team also plays one additional game against a team from the other conference.

1 game

Add it all up (6+4+2+4+1) and you'll see that each NFL team plays 17 games.

In order to make sure that each of the 32 teams gets a chance to play games against each other, the matchups of divisions are rotated on regular cycles: three years for other divisions in the same conference and four years for divisions in the other conference.

TWO-MINUTE WARNING

In the early days of the NFL, the fans, the players, and the coaches couldn't trust the stadium clock to know how much time was left to play. The official game clock was actually a watch held by one of the officials. The clocks in each stadium only gave a rough estimate of how much time was actually remaining. So the NFL instituted a two-minute warning where the referee would stop the clock near the end of the first half, and then again near the end of the game, and let both teams know exactly how much time was remaining. By the 1960s, the stadium clock had become the game's official clock, but the two-minute warning was such an important strategic moment that the NFL kept it. In the CFL, there is a three-minute warning.

PENCIL POWER

Every football game has two halves. Each of those halves is divided into two quarters, so there are four quarters in a game. Each of those quarters has 15 minutes of actual playing time. So how many minutes of playing time are there in a game?

ANSWER: 4 quarters x 15 minutes in a quarter = 60 total minutes of playing time

STOP THE CLOCK

In addition to the two-minute warning, every team in an NFL game gets three time-outs per half where they can stop the clock (reasons for taking a time-out include to break up the other team's momentum, talk about possible plays, or discuss strategy). There are other ways to stop the clock—10, in fact, according to the NFL rule book. Most often you'll see the clock stop when a team scores on a play, when the ball goes out of bounds, or when a pass is thrown but not caught. The clock also stops when there's a penalty. Penalties are called when someone on the field breaks the rules. The punishment is usually that the ball will be moved 5, 10, or 15 yards up or down the field, depending on which team is penalized.

THE NEW ORLEANS SAINTS BATTLE THE LOS ANGELES RAMS IN A 2019 PLAYOFF GAME.

KANSAS CITY CHIEFS QUARTERBACK PATRICK MAHOMES SIGNALS FOR A TIME-OUT.

TRY *THIS!*

Schedule Mania

When all the games in an NFL season are added up, there's a total of 272 games on the schedule, which take place over 18 weeks. Five different NFL executives work to create the schedule. Hundreds of different computers are used to produce thousands of possible matchups. Then the five executives have to figure out the best possible schedule for each team. They have to juggle issues such as what games need to be on TV, or when there's another event (such as a concert) booked at a popular football stadium. Do you think you could do it?

Clearly, it's pretty hard to make a schedule ... but not all of it takes a computer to figure out. One thing you need to know is that each NFL schedule is based on the standings from the previous season. Using the model NFL standings on the right, you should be able to determine which teams the Pittsburgh Steelers would play the next season.

Here are the key points to keep in mind (and go back to page 18 if you need a schedule refresher):

1 Pittsburgh plays in the AFC North in the American Football Conference. Pittsburgh has to play one home game and one road game against each team in its own division.

2 Pittsburgh plays one game against all four teams in another division in its own conference.

3 Pittsburgh plays one game against one team from the two other divisions in its own conference. (When matching up against the other divisions, teams always play against a team that finished in the same spot in the standings ... so be sure to note where the Steelers rank.)

PITTSBURGH STEELERS PLAYERS

4 Pittsburgh plays one game against all four teams in another division in the other conference. (Assume that the rotation of divisions has Pittsburgh playing against the teams in the NFC East this year.)

5 Pittsburgh plays one game against a team from the other conference that finished in the same position in the standings in a division that isn't already on its schedule.

Plan It Out

Can you pick out the 12 teams the Steelers would play? And how many games against each? Don't worry about which games will be played at home and which will be on the road. Each team's record is given after its name (wins–losses). Good luck!

American Football Conference	National Football Conference
AFC EAST	**NFC EAST**
New England Patriots 12–4	Dallas Cowboys 9–7
Buffalo Bills 10–6	Philadelphia Eagles 7–9
New York Jets 8–8	Washington Commanders 6–10
Miami Dolphins 6–10	New York Giants 4–12
AFC NORTH	**NFC NORTH**
Baltimore Ravens 12–4	Green Bay Packers 11–5
Pittsburgh Steelers 10-6	Minnesota Vikings 10–6
Cleveland Browns 5–11	Chicago Bears 7–9
Cincinnati Bengals 3–13	Detroit Lions 6–10
AFC SOUTH	**NFC SOUTH**
Houston Texans 9–7	New Orleans Saints 14–2
Indianapolis Colts 8–8	Tampa Bay Buccaneers 8–8
Tennessee Titans 5–11	Carolina Panthers 7–9
Jacksonville Jaguars 3–13	Atlanta Falcons 7–9
AFC WEST	**NFC WEST**
Los Angeles Chargers 12–4	San Francisco 49ers 13–3
Kansas City Chiefs 11–5	Seattle Seahawks 10–6
Las Vegas Raiders 7–9	Los Angeles Rams 7–9
Denver Broncos 4–12	Arizona Cardinals 5–11

ANSWER: The Steelers play two games against the Baltimore Ravens, Cleveland Browns, and Cincinnati Bengals from their own division. They play one game against the New England Patriots, Buffalo Bills, New York Jets, and Miami Dolphins from the AFC East. Pittsburgh faces the Indianapolis Colts and the Kansas City Chiefs from the other divisions (South and West) in the AFC. They also meet up with the Dallas Cowboys, Philadelphia Eagles, Washington Commanders, and New York Giants from the NFC East for one game each. Their final game would be against either Minnesota, Tampa Bay, or Seattle.

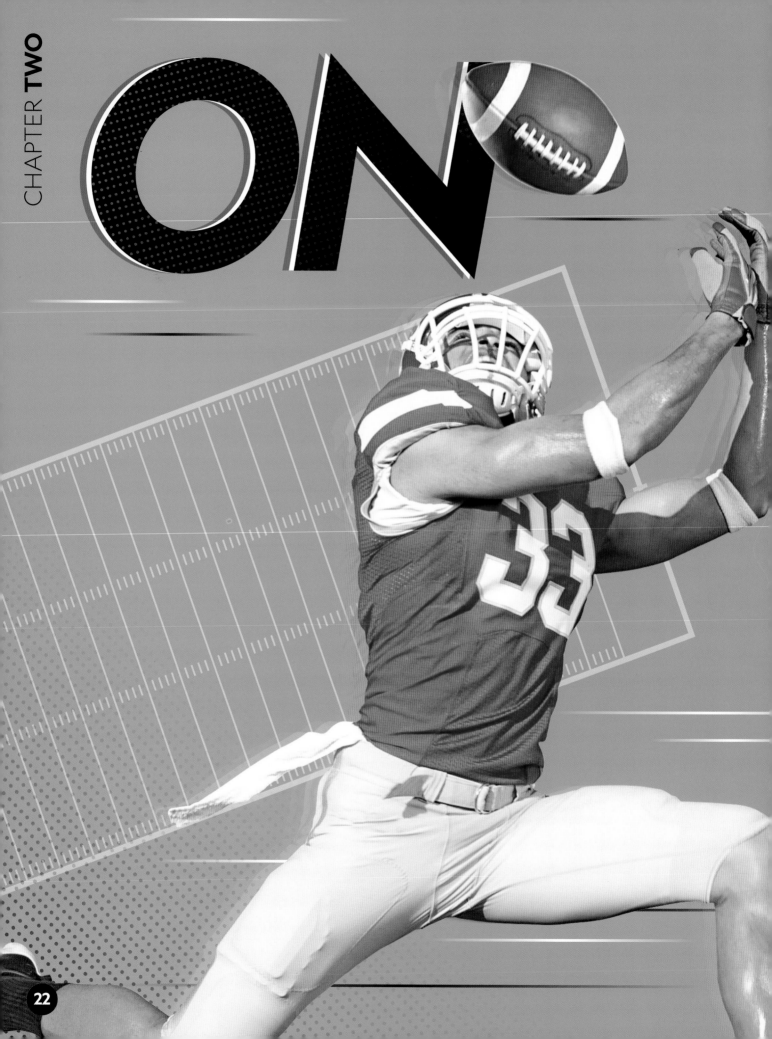

CHAPTER TWO

ON

THE FIELD

While it may look like a simple field, there's a lot happening on the green. That field is full of more than just lines and numbers. It's where all the action happens. We'll run through all those lines, count up the large digits, and find out exactly who's on the field, too. Ready, break!

HISTORY BY THE NUMBERS

Most images of early American football teams show that players wore jerseys with just one solid color or with stripes. Sometimes they wore a letter on the front of those jerseys: H for Harvard, Y for Yale, or P for Pittsburgh. Players on early NFL teams wore numbers, but only on the backs of their jerseys. In 1929, the Green Bay Packers began wearing numbers on the front. While the Packers' numbers were very small, players on every NFL team since the championship Chicago Bears in 1932 have worn large numbers on the front and back of their jerseys.

THE 1929 GREEN BAY PACKERS

MARKING THE FIELD

American football is traditionally played on a field that's 100 yards long from goal line to goal line. There are also two end zones that are each 10 yards deep, so the entire field is 120 yards long. Let's look at the NFL field, where the highest level of football is played.

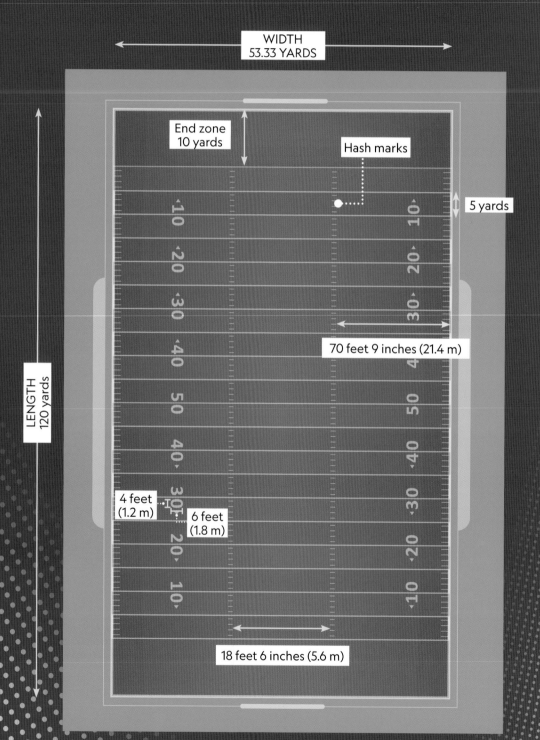

WIDTH
53.33 YARDS

End zone
10 yards

Hash marks

5 yards

70 feet 9 inches (21.4 m)

LENGTH
120 yards

4 feet
(1.2 m)

6 feet
(1.8 m)

18 feet 6 inches (5.6 m)

STAT STORY

The very first rule in the NFL rule book—Rule 1, Section 1, Article 1—provides details on the length and the width of a football field. In 2011, the NFL noticed some colorful changes happening in college football and added something new to Article 1: "The surface of the entire Field of Play must be a League-approved shade of green." Some football fields use artificial turf, a type of plastic grass, that comes in a few colors. In fact, the artificial turf field at Boise State University in Idaho, U.S.A., is colored a deep blue and is known as "Smurf Turf" after the blue-colored cartoon characters. Because of this, some people call the NFL's green field rule the Boise State Rule.

THE BLUE "SMURF TURF" AT BOISE STATE

DIGIT-YOU-KNOW?

Each new down begins with the ball placed on the field somewhere on or in between the hash marks. If the previous play ends somewhere between those hash marks, the ball is placed on that spot. If a play ends outside either of the hash marks, then the ball is brought back and placed on the field in line with the hash marks on that side of the field. In the NFL, the hash marks are lined up with the outer edges of the goal posts. They are placed 70 feet 9 inches (21.4 m) from the sidelines on either side, and there is 18 feet 6 inches (5.6 m) of space between them. One of the only differences between an NFL field and a college football field is the position of the hash marks. In NCAA football, the hash marks are spread out wider. They are only 60 feet (18.2 m) from the sidelines, and there is 40 feet (12.2 m) of space between them.

LINE 'EM UP

Let's look closely at the lines and numbers on the football field. You don't actually see a 100 on the field, but 50 yards in both directions from midfield adds up to 100. So how did a football field come to be 100 yards long? And have you ever heard someone refer to a football field as a gridiron? Let's find out why.

BIGGER WASN'T BETTER

In the 1870s, football fields were enormous. They were 140 yards long and 70 yards wide. You needed a pretty big space to be able to play. In 1881, the rules were changed to reduce the field to 110 yards long and 53 ⅓ yards wide. In terms of total area, this cut the size almost in half.

But in 1912, the rules changed again. That's when the first official end zones were created. Before that, there was often just a goal line at either end of the field. When the decision was made to add these 10-yard end zones, a lot of stadiums didn't have space for them. So, in order to accommodate them, the size of the playing field was reduced again. This time it was cut by 10 yards from 110 to 100.

The field size hasn't changed since 1912 ... so it looks like 100 yards was a perfect score!

THE END ZONE ADDS 10 YARDS AT EACH END OF THE FIELD.

CANADIAN STADIUMS ARE SMALLER, BUT THE FIELD IS LARGER.

OH, CANADA!

In Canadian football, the playing field is still 110 yards long instead of 100 and the two end zones are each 20 yards deep. That's 150 yards in total. Canadian fields are wider, too. They're 65 yards across, compared to American fields, which are only 53 ⅓ yards wide.

PENCIL POWER

You've read about length and width, but what about area? To calculate the area of a rectangle, which is the shape of a football field, you need to multiply length by width. Area is measured in square units. Here's the formula:

L (length in units) × W (width in units) = Area (in units squared)

Given the lengths and widths of these fields in yards, what are their areas in square yards (without the end zones)?

A modern American football field: L is 100, W is 53.33
A Canadian football field: L is 110, W is 65
A football field from the 1870s: L is 140, W is 70

ANSWER: American field:
100 × 53.33 = 5,333 square yards
Canadian field:
110 × 65 = 7,150 square yards
1870s football field:
140 × 70 = 9,800 square yards

GRIDIRON

People often refer to a football field as a gridiron. In fact, in many countries where soccer is known as football, they refer to the game played in North America as gridiron football.

The word "gridiron" dates back to the 1300s and was commonly used to describe a metal grill for cooking food over a fire. Even today, those long yard lines every five yards that run right across a football field make it resemble a cooking grill. However, a true grid doesn't just have lines across its width. A grid also has lines that run along its length. Well, there once was a time when American football fields had lines across their lengths, too.

Early rules about passing required players to keep track of distance. To make it easier to see those distances, football fields had grid lines dividing them up into five-yard squares. Some people thought those old fields looked like giant checkerboards. Soon, the rules about passing changed and the extra "checkerboard" lines were removed.

THE RED ZONE

If you're watching a football game on television, you'll likely hear an announcer refer to the "red zone" at some point during the broadcast. Although it's not generally marked in any way—it certainly isn't red—the red zone refers to the two areas of the field between the 20-yard lines and the nearest goal lines. When a team has the ball inside the red zone, its chances of scoring a touchdown are high because it's so close to the goal line.

OFFENSE VS. DEFENSE

As we learned in chapter one, the standard lineup in American football has 11 players on each team playing on the field. Although some of them have similar names, the positions on offense and defense are quite different. As those players battle up and down the field, you'll often hear announcers on TV or radio using numbers to describe where the action is taking place.

QB TOM BRADY PREPARES TO PASS.

11 ON OFFENSE

When the team has possession of the ball and is trying to score, they are on offense. The standard offensive lineup has seven positions along the line of scrimmage. The center, or the man in the middle, is the one who snaps the ball to begin each play. The players on either side of the center are called guards. Next to the guards are the tackles. Collectively, these five players along the line of scrimmage are known as the offensive line. Their main job is to block defensive players.

The position next to the offensive tackles, lined up as the last players on the line of scrimmage, is called the end. Teams are allowed to have two ends (one on each end of the scrimmage line) but often they'll use just one, who is known as a tight end. When there's only one end, the other player who lines up on the line of scrimmage is usually a wide receiver. Teams can also use two wide receivers and no tight ends at all. Offensive players who line up behind the line of scrimmage are known as the backfield. These players usually include the quarterback and running backs, or tailbacks.

11 ON DEFENSE

On defense, teams traditionally use four players on the line of scrimmage: two tackles and two ends. Together, the tackles and ends are known as the defensive linemen. Behind them is a middle linebacker and two outside linebackers. Sometimes, a team will use four linebackers and only three defensive linemen. In those cases, there will be two defensive ends on either side of a player in the middle who is known as a nose guard or a nose tackle. Generally, the defensive team will have four defensive backs, who are known collectively as the secondary. There are usually two cornerbacks who line up outside of the linebackers and two safeties lined up farther back.

THE RAMS DEFENSE SACKS THE BRONCOS' QB.

PLAY YOUR POSITION

These abbreviations are commonly used to note each player's position:

QB	**Quarterback**
RB	Running back
HB	**Halfback**
TB	Tailback
FB	**Fullback**
LG/RG	Left guard/Right guard
OT	**Offensive tackle**
LT/RT	Left tackle/Right tackle
TE	**Tight end**
WR	Wide receiver
DT	**Defensive tackle**
DE	Defensive end
LB	**Linebacker**
DB	Defensive back
CB	**Cornerback**
S	Safety
PK	**Placekicker**
P	Punter
K	**Kicker**

THE **THIRD TEAM**

Every game has two teams, but there's also another team out there. They're the game officials wearing black and white stripes. These officials, sometimes called zebras, have one head official—the referee—working with six other officials. It's the job of the zebras to make sure the other two teams play by the rules. When officials see a player break a rule, they throw a small flag on the play to indicate a penalty. Most penalties result in moving the football toward the offending team's end zone, usually by 5, 10, or 15 yards. A penalty also almost always wipes out any gains a team has made on a play.

REFEREE
The referee has control over the whole game. He or she makes all the signals and announcements about penalties during the game. There are 36 different arm actions that the referee can make to indicate different penalties, scoring plays, first downs, and changes to the clock. The other game officials wear black hats, but the referee wears a white hat.

UMPIRE
The main role of the umpire is to rule on players' conduct and actions along the line of scrimmage. Most umpires line up 12 yards into the offensive backfield and one or two yards outside the tight end.

DOWN JUDGE
The down judge is responsible for making sure players are in their proper position along the line of scrimmage before each down. Once the play begins, the down judge is responsible for determining if a player goes out of bounds at the sidelines.

SIDE JUDGE
The side judge keeps time as a backup to the clock operator. This official also rules on plays involving receivers.

DOWN JUDGE SARAH THOMAS WITH ODELL BECKHAM.

FIELD JUDGE
The field judge rules on plays involving the receivers—the players who catch the ball. He or she assists on covering the actions of the runners.

BACK JUDGE
The back judge lines up 25 yards down field from the offense. He or she focuses on the tight end and running backs and on the defensive players covering them.

LINE JUDGE
The line judge has the main responsibility for making sure that a quarterback is behind the line of scrimmage when throwing a forward pass. The line judge is also responsible for calls along the line of scrimmage.

FLAG ON THE PLAY

Here are some of the most common penalties called in football, and the number of yards they'll cost a team:

CLIPPING
A player contacting a non-ball-carrying opponent from behind and at or below the waist—15 yards

ENCROACHMENT
When a defensive player crosses the line of scrimmage and contacts an offensive player or the ball before the ball has been snapped (called "offside" in Canadian football)—5 yards

FACE MASK
When a player grabs the face mask of another player while trying to block or tackle him—15 yards

FALSE START
When an offensive player moves illegally before the ball is snapped (called "illegal procedure" in Canadian football)—5 yards

HOLDING
Grasping or pulling an opponent who is not the ballcarrier—10 yards

PASS INTERFERENCE (DEFENSE)
Making physical contact with a receiver after the ball has been thrown and before it has been touched by another player—Automatic first down

PASS INTERFERENCE (OFFENSE)
Making physical contact with a defensive player after the ball has been thrown and before it has been touched by another player—10 yards

UNSPORTSMANLIKE CONDUCT
When a person acts or speaks in a way that is rude, mean, unfair, or dangerous on purpose—15 yards

JENNIFER KING

HISTORY BY THE NUMBERS
On September 27, 2020, when the Cleveland Browns hosted the Washington Commanders, it marked the first time in NFL history that two female coaches worked a game with a female official, too. Callie Brownson was the chief of staff for Cleveland, while Jennifer King was a running backs coach for Washington. Sarah Thomas was in the game as a sideline official.

CALLIE BROWNSON

WEAR IT WELL!

If you're playing catch, you don't need much more than a football. But as soon as you get into serious play, and certainly before you tackle, you're going to need some very specific equipment.

WHAT TO WEAR

According to the NFL rule book, there are seven items of equipment or clothing that each player has to wear:

1 Helmet, with face protector (face mask) attached

2 Jersey

3 Numerals (numbers on your jersey)

4 Pants

5 Shoulder pads, thigh pads, and knee pads

6 Stockings

7 Shoes

The rules for high school and college football include a few extra required items, like hip pads and mouth guards.

If you were an NFL player packing your equipment bag, here are some other things you might need:

1 A T-shirt (to wear under your team jersey)

2 Gloves (to help you grip the ball better)

3 Rib protectors

4 Wrist bands

5 A towel (Some players—often the center—tuck a towel into their pants to dry off their hands.)

6 A cap or headband for under your helmet

7 A mouth guard

WHAT'S YOUR NUMBER?

Every player has to wear a number on their jersey. These numbers not only help fans identify their favorite players, they also help officials make sure that everyone is lined up in the proper place. Players' numbers are selected according to position in the NFL. Starting in 2021, running backs, wide receivers, tight ends, defensive backs, and linebackers all have a lot of flexibility in the numbers they can choose. Here are the guidelines:

Quarterback: 1–19

Running back: 1–49, 80–89

Wide receiver/tight end: 1–49, 80–89

Offensive line: 50–79

Defensive line: 50–79, 90–99

Linebacker: 1–59, 90–99

Defensive back: 1–49

Kicker/punter: 1–19

The CFL uses a similar numbering system to the NFL, but in NCAA football, the system is a little different. There are actually no special numbers required for defensive players, but these numbers are recommended for offense:

Quarterback and running back: 1–49

Center: 50–59

Guard: 60–69

Tackle: 70–79

End and wide receiver: 80–99

PROTECT YOURSELF

Football is a rough game with high-speed collisions that can lead to injuries. Even with new technologies, football players are still vulnerable to head injuries such as concussions. A concussion is a serious injury suffered by the brain. Concussions can be caused by a bump, blow, or jolt to the head, but they can also occur when the body is hit in a way that causes the head to move back and forth rapidly.

Modern football helmets are designed to help protect against head injuries. Today's helmets have an outer shell of polycarbonate plastic. The shell can be as thin as just 3.35 millimeters. Polycarbonates are lightweight but very strong. They can help spread out the force of any impact so the load can be absorbed by other elements inside the helmet. Those elements include polyurethane foam pads, which are strong but very flexible. Today's football helmets often include foam air pockets. The pads and air pockets help absorb the energy of a hit.

Even with protection, a concussion can occur, and, even after it heals, it can lead to more serious problems in the future. So be careful out there, and always wear your helmet!

SCIENCE STUFF

A helmet reduces the peak force from a hit that is transferred to the head by temporarily storing or spreading impact energy. The foam part inside of a helmet crushes, which absorbs the energy from the impact and extends the time it takes for your head to stop by about six-thousandths—.006—of a second. That doesn't sound like much, but it can make a huge difference in terms of the impact on your brain.

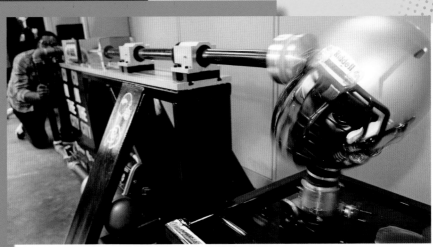

HAVING A BALL

Most leagues have very specific rules about the footballs they use. A football must be made from four leather panels that are stitched together to form the surface. Although you'll sometimes hear people refer to a football as a "pigskin," there's no pig here. The leather that is used is actually made from cowhide. It must have small bumps on the surface, which make the ball a little easier to grip.

All leather footballs have laces. In the old days, these laces were used to help hold the ball together. These days, the laces are really just for show ... though they can make the football a little bit easier to grip, too.

Inside the four leather panels is a rubber bladder which is inflated to give the ball its size and shape. That shape is formally referred to as a "prolate spheroid," but you're more likely to refer to it as an oval, or as egg shaped.

SCIENCE STUFF

League rules in the NFL, the CFL, and the NCAA all say that the bladder inside each football is to be inflated to about 12.5 to 13.5 pounds per square inch. If a ball is deflated a little bit it will be softer and easier to grip, which can make it slightly easier to throw for short passes. An underinflated ball is also much easier to catch because it's less likely to bounce off a receiver's fingers. Pounds per square inch—or psi for short—is a unit of pressure. It's the pressure resulting from a force of one pound applied to an area of one square inch. Divide the pounds of perpendicular force by the square inches of area on which it is acting to get the pressure in pounds per square inch.

MEASURING THE PIGSKIN

The footballs used in the CFL used to be slightly larger than NFL footballs, but now the rules of both leagues give the same dimensions:

Long axis:	11 to 11 ¼ inches
Long circumference:	28 to 28 ½ inches
Short circumference:	21 to 21 ¼ inches
Weight:	14 to 15 ounces

NCAA footballs are slightly smaller:

Long axis:	10 ⅞ to 11 ⁷⁄₁₆ inches
Long circumference:	27 ¾ to 28 ½ inches
Short circumference:	20 ¾ to 21 ¼ inches
Weight:	14 to 15 ounces

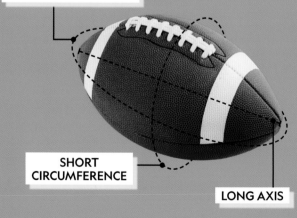

LONG CIRCUMFERENCE

SHORT CIRCUMFERENCE

LONG AXIS

STRIPES & COLORS

All official footballs are a light brown color that the NFL and NCAA rule books call "natural tan." There are no stripes on an NFL football. The CFL ball has two one-inch (2.54-cm)-wide white stripes circling all four leather panels. NCAA footballs also have a pair of one-inch-wide white stripes, but they only cover the two leather panels on either side of the laces.

DIGIT-YOU-KNOW?

Both teams in an NFL game must provide 12 primary and 12 backup balls to be used in a game no later than two hours and 30 minutes before the game starts. Also, six more brand-new balls are shipped directly to the stadium by the company that makes them. They are used in the kicking game.

DEFLATEGATE

Before the AFC Championship game between the New England Patriots and Indianapolis Colts on January 18, 2015, the Colts notified the NFL that they believed the Patriots were using underinflated balls. The Patriots won the game 45–7, but it was later confirmed that nearly all the balls that New England used during the game were inflated below 12 psi (and not the required 12.5 to 13.5 psi).

After a lengthy investigation, New England QB Tom Brady was suspended for the first four games of the 2016 NFL season. The Patriots were fined one million dollars and lost two draft picks. The entire affair has become known as "Deflategate."

UMPIRE CARL PAGANELLI HOLDS ONTO A BALL DURING THE 2015 AFC CHAMPIONSHIP GAME.

TRY *THIS!*

Getting Out on the Field

Watching football on TV with your friends or family can be lots of fun. Throwing around a football with your friends in a park or a backyard can be even more exciting.

You'll need a football to try this drill, but you don't need a real football field—only some open space and at least one other person. Depending on how good a throwing arm you've got, you can start off as close as five yards (4.6 m) apart. If you're not on a real football field with yard lines, you can pace off five long steps. Then just start throwing the ball back and forth. Don't whip it at each other, as you want to be able to catch it.

After you've gotten the hang of it, take a step back after each throw and catch. If there's only two of you, keep track of how many passes you complete and how far apart you get before someone drops the ball, and then try to break that record. If there are four or more of you, turn it into a competition. Keep track of which pair completes the most passes in a row, and they'll be the winners.

Head back out another day and try again. How do your stats compare?

CHAPTER THREE

THE PASSING

GAME

No single player can win a football game alone. The different players on offense have to work together to move the ball up the field and into the end zone. Even so, to really master the passing game, your team must have a good quarterback.

The quarterback, or QB, barks out the signals that get each play started. The QB has to know the responsibilities of every player on offense and scan the defense for weaknesses. A quarterback needs great physical skills—a strong arm helps—but there has to be a lot going on in his head, too. In addition to using his own skills, he also has to inspire and lead his teammates.

As important as the quarterback is, a QB needs someone to throw the ball to. So in this chapter we'll also take a look at the all-important receivers.

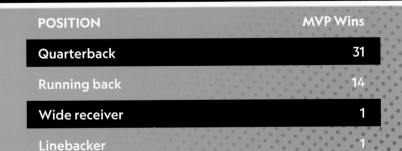

DIGIT-YOU-KNOW?

The Professional Football Writers of America selects a Most Valuable Player (MVP) in the NFL at the end of the season. Through the 2020 season, a total of 47 winners have been selected. Nearly two out of every three winners have been quarterbacks.

POSITION	MVP Wins
Quarterback	31
Running back	14
Wide receiver	1
Linebacker	1

ALL ABOUT THE PASS

There are a lot of statistics used to measure the success of a quarterback and the passing game. Before we tackle those stats, here are some key terms, a bit of science, and even a handful of history that is helpful to know.

FORWARD PASS

A forward pass is any pass thrown from behind the line of scrimmage that moves forward (closer to the opponent's goal line) after leaving the passer's hand.

CINCINNATI'S JOE BURROW

HISTORY BY THE NUMBERS

Where did the quarterback name come from? Think about coins. A quarter—25 cents—is worth one-quarter or 25 percent of a dollar. The player who lined up in the backfield the farthest behind the line of scrimmage was known as a "fullback". The player who lined up halfway between the line of scrimmage and the fullback was known as a "halfback." So it was decided that the player who was positioned between the halfback and the line of scrimmage should be known as the "quarterback."

ATTEMPT

Any time a quarterback throws the ball down the field, that's a pass attempt. During the 2020 season, Tom Brady of the Tampa Bay Buccaneers became the new all-time career leader in pass attempts. The all-time single-season leader is Matthew Stafford. Stafford had 727 pass attempts with the Detroit Lions in 2012.

TOM BRADY OF TAMPA BAY

A COMPLETION TO MICHAEL THOMAS

COMPLETION/ RECEPTION/INCOMPLETE

When a quarterback throws the ball and it's caught by one of his teammates, that's called a completion. The receiver who catches the ball is credited with a reception. If the ball isn't caught, it's incomplete. Drew Brees is the career leader in completions with 7,142, as well as the single-season completion leader with a record 471 set in 2016.

LATERAL

A lateral is a pass that goes backward or sideways to a teammate. A lateral pass can be thrown anywhere on the football field—as long as the ball is not thrown forward. A lateral is often thrown underhand.

INTERCEPTION

An interception is when a quarterback throws the ball and it's caught by a member of the defensive team. Often, when a ball is intercepted, an announcer on TV or radio will say the pass has been "picked off." That's why interceptions are informally called "picks." If a defensive player intercepts the ball and runs with it into the other team's end zone, people call that a "pick 6" because the defensive team scores six points for the touchdown.

SCIENCE STUFF

Because a football isn't round, it is thrown horizontally, with its longest part almost parallel to the ground. This helps the football slice through the air. A rotational spin applied to the ball by flicking the wrist to give it a spiral motion reduces air resistance and allows the throw to be more accurate. Though the angle at which the ball is thrown can make a big difference, the harder a football is thrown, the farther it will go. The velocity, or speed, at which the ball is thrown gives it energy to fly down the field. This energy is created by the strength of the quarterback's arm and is transferred to the football.

The angle at which the ball is thrown can be referred to as the "launch angle." The larger the launch angle, the higher the ball will go. Throw it too high, and the arc of the ball will look more like a rainbow than a flat arc. A little extra height might help it go farther downfield, but it also gives a defensive player more time to get in the way. A straighter pass is tougher to defend. Still, there are times when a quarterback needs to throw at a higher angle to get the ball over a defender and safely down to his receiver.

MEASURING PASSES

To get first downs and score touchdowns, offensive players need to gain yards. Passing the football is one way to do it. Game by game and season by season, the yards pile up. There's no fancy math needed to figure out how many yards a quarterback has thrown—only arithmetic. Simply add up the total yards gained on every pass that a QB completes.

JOE BURROW

ADDING IT UP

Okay, so we said it wasn't fancy math, but in truth there is one tricky part to adding up the yards a quarterback has thrown. It doesn't actually matter how far the ball flies through the air. If a QB throws the ball as short as even one yard in the air, but the receiver who catches it runs for 10 yards, or 20, or even 99, the quarterback's passing yards include all the total yardage from that play. Confused? Don't be.

Let's say, for example, that a QB throws the ball 12 yards in the air past the line of scrimmage, and his receiver gets tackled as soon as he catches it. The QB will be credited with 12 passing yards for that play. However, if the quarterback only throws a pass 5 yards, but his receiver catches it and runs for 10 more yards, the total for that play is 15 yards (5 + 10), and the QB is credited with 15 passing yards.

HOW FAR?

Generally speaking, experts say that an NFL QB can throw the ball 60 yards with accuracy during a game but slightly farther in practice (when there's less pressure and the defense isn't as a tough). Before quarterback Patrick Mahomes of the Kansas City Chiefs was a star in the NFL, he played college football at Texas Tech. Mahomes once told an interviewer that he threw the ball almost 80 yards while working out before a college game, and there's video to prove it. And long before Lamar Jackson played with the Baltimore Ravens, there was a video of him from a practice in high school that showed him throwing a ball 100 yards in the air. That's all the way from one goal line to the other!

PATRICK MAHOMES

STATSTARS

The Canadian Football League record for career passing yards is held by Anthony Calvillo, who played in the CFL for 20 seasons from 1994 to 2013. Mainly a star with the Montreal Alouettes, Calvillo threw for 79,816 yards. He never played in the NFL, but until the 2020 season his career total topped every quarterback in NFL history.

PENCIL POWER

Lamar Jackson started his first game for the Baltimore Ravens on November 18, 2018. He threw 19 passes with 13 completions and one interception. Based on the stats below, can you determine how many yards Jackson passed for? Remember: Simply add up all the yards. Note: If the pass was incomplete or there was no play because a penalty was called, then you don't have to count anything at all.

1ST QUARTER: Pass complete for 4 yards
Pass incomplete
Pass complete for 0 yards

2ND QUARTER: Pass complete for 9 yards
Pass complete for 7 yards
Pass complete for 16 yards
Penalty—no play
Pass incomplete
Pass complete for 9 yards
Pass complete for 8 yards
Pass complete for 23 yards
Pass incomplete

3RD QUARTER: Pass intercepted
Pass complete for 16 yards
Pass incomplete
Pass complete for 17 yards
Pass incomplete
Pass complete for 14 yards

4TH QUARTER: Pass complete for 19 yards
Pass complete for 8 yards

ANSWER: 4 + 0 + 9 + 7 + 16 + 9 + 8 + 23 + 16 + 17 + 14 + 19 + 8 = 150 yards

LAMAR JACKSON

PEYTON MANNING

LEAGUE LEADERS

Here's a look at some of the greatest passing performances in NFL history by quarterbacks and wide receivers.

QUARTERBACKS:

All-time leader in passing yards: Career	
Tom Brady (2000–October 24, 2021)	81,479 yards

All-time leader in passing yards: Season	
Peyton Manning (Denver Broncos, 2013)	5,477 yards

All-time leader in passing yards: Game	
Norm Van Brocklin (Los Angeles Rams, 1951)	554 yards

WIDE RECEIVERS:

All-time leader in receiving yards: Career	
Jerry Rice (1985–2004)	22,895 yards

All-time leader in receiving yards: Season	
Calvin Johnson (Detroit Lions, 2012)	1,964 yards

All-time leader in receiving yards: Game	
Flipper Anderson (Los Angeles Rams, 1989)	336 yards

CALVIN JOHNSON

PASSER RATING:
PLAYING THE PERCENTAGES

The NFL rates its passers using a complicated system that compares passing statistics dating back to 1960. It provides a single number that can be used to see how well a quarterback has done. This is not a perfect statistic because it only rates one thing—passing skills. It doesn't account for leadership or any other attributes that make a quarterback great.

Passer rating can be worked out for a single game, an entire season, or a whole career. It is based on a formula combining four other basic statistics: completion percentage, touchdown percentage, interception percentage, and average yards per pass. We'll learn how to compile those numbers here, but figuring out a quarterback's passer rating number is actually really complicated. Statisticians take the results of these four basic stats and put them into a lengthy mathematical formula that subtracts set numbers in some places and multiplies with fractions in others before converting everything into a standard scale. Complicated, right? Not to worry—let's look at the pieces we know you can tackle and leave the rest to the professional statisticians.

COMPLETION PERCENTAGE

To figure out this stat, you need to divide the number of passes a quarterback has completed by the number of passes he's attempted. During the time he starred in the NFL with the Indianapolis Colts and then the Denver Broncos from 1998 to 2015, Peyton Manning threw 9,380 passes in his career. He completed 6,125 of them.

Here's the formula for completion percentage:

(Passes completed ÷ Passes attempted) × 100

So for Peyton Manning: 6,125 ÷ 9,380 = .652985

.652985 × 100 = 65.2985

His percentage completion rounds off to 65.30%.

ROUNDING OFF
When there are a lot of numbers after a decimal point—as with .652985—it's common to round them off. When doing so, the last number kept should be increased by one if the next number is 5 or higher. In the NFL, most numbers are rounded to two decimal points. So 65.2985 becomes 65.30.

TOUCHDOWN PERCENTAGE

You can't win if you don't score, so touchdowns are pretty important. Even though Sid Luckman, star quarterback of the Chicago Bears from 1939 to 1950, didn't throw a lot of touchdown passes in his career compared to modern quarterbacks, he's still the all-time leader in touchdown percentage. Luckman attempted 1,744 passes in his career and threw 137 touchdown passes.

Here's the formula for touchdown percentage:

(Touchdown passes ÷ Passes attempted) × 100

So for Sid Luckman: 137 ÷ 1,744 = .078555

.078555 × 100 = 7.8555

That's a touchdown percentage that rounds off to 7.86%.

AVERAGE YARD PER PASS

To find the average yard per pass, you divide a quarterback's total yards passing by the number of times he threw the ball. Like Sid Luckman, Otto Graham, who played with the Cleveland Browns from 1946 to 1955, didn't throw a lot of passes compared to modern quarterbacks, but he's still the career leader in average yards per pass. He threw 1,565 passes and completed them for 13,499 yards.

Here's the formula for average yards per pass:

Yards passing ÷ Passes attempted

So for Otto Graham: 13,499 ÷ 1,565 = 8.62555

His average yards per pass rounds off to 8.63 yards.

INTERCEPTION PERCENTAGE

Throwing an interception—which gives the other team possession of the ball—is one of the worst things a quarterback can do. So, when it comes to interception percentage, the lowest number is the best number because it means the quarterback hasn't thrown that many interceptions. Former San Francisco 49ers star Steve Young has one of the lowest interception percentages among all quarterbacks in the Pro Football Hall of Fame. Young threw 4,149 passes in his career and had 107 of them intercepted.

Here's the formula for interception percentage:

(Interceptions thrown ÷ Passes attempted) × 100

So for Steve Young: 107 ÷ 4,149 = .025789

0.025789 × 100 = 2.5789

His interception percentage rounds off to 2.58%.

PENCIL POWER

John Elway was a star quarterback with the Denver Broncos from 1983 to 1998. During his career, Elway attempted 7,250 passes. Of those, he completed 4,123 passes for 51,475 yards passing with 300 touchdown passes and 226 interceptions. Using the formulas shown for each category, can you figure out Elway's completion percentage, touchdown percentage, interception percentage, and average yards per pass? (Remember to round off your answers to two decimal places.)

ANSWERS:
Completion percentage: 4,123 ÷ 7,250 = .56868 × 100 = 56.868 .... 56.87%
Touchdown percentage: 300 ÷ 7,250 = .04137 × 100 = 4.137 ... 4.14%
Interception percentage: 226 ÷ 7,250 = .03117 × 100 = 3.117 ... 3.12%
Average yards per pass: 51,475 ÷ 7,250 = 7.10

45

The biggest stars in football history are all honored in halls of fame. The five NFL quarterbacks highlighted here are members of the Pro Football Hall of Fame in Canton, Ohio, U.S.A. The CFL star is a member of the Canadian Football Hall of Fame in Hamilton, Ontario. These players span many different eras, but each of them put up impressive numbers during their careers and were considered among the best players of their day.

2 DOUG FLUTIE

Jersey numbers: 2, 20, 22
Years in CFL: 1990–1997
Year inducted into Hall of Fame: 2008

Doug Flutie was an NCAA star at Boston College and also spent 12 years in the NFL, but his eight seasons in the CFL made him one of the greatest players in Canadian football history. Flutie played with the British Columbia Lions, Calgary Stampeders, and Toronto Argonauts. He was named the CFL's Most Outstanding Player six times and led his team to three Grey Cup championships. Flutie holds all-time CFL single-season records for most yards passing (6,619 in 1991) and most touchdown passes (48 in 1994).

10 FRAN TARKENTON

Jersey number: 10
Years in NFL: 1961–1978
Year inducted into Hall of Fame: 1986

Fran Tarkenton made an instant impression in the NFL. Making his debut with the Minnesota Vikings in the team's first game in franchise history, he threw four touchdown passes in a 37–13 win over the Chicago Bears. At the time of his retirement, he led all NFL passers in attempts (6,467), completions (3,686), yards (47,003), and touchdowns (342). Tarkenton was also a great scrambler who ran for 3,674 yards and scored 32 touchdowns.

12 JOE NAMATH

Jersey number: 12
Years in NFL: 1965–1977
Year inducted into Hall of Fame: 1985

Joe Namath signed with the New York Jets in 1965 when the American Football League was a rival league of the NFL. Namath's contract paid him $400,000 over three years, which was the richest rookie contract in football history—and maybe all of sports history—at that time. Namath would lead the Jets to a stunning upset of the Baltimore Colts in Super Bowl III in 1969.

13 KURT WARNER

Jersey number: 13
Years in NFL: 1998–2009
Year inducted into Hall of Fame: 2017

Kurt Warner was never drafted by an NFL team and worked in a grocery store after his college football career. He later played three seasons in the Arena Football League and one season in Europe before joining the St. Louis Rams in 1998. A year later, Warner led the Rams to a Super Bowl championship, setting what was then a Super Bowl record with 414 passing yards.

33 SAMMY BAUGH

Jersey number: 33
Years in NFL: 1937–1952
Year inducted into Hall of Fame: 1963

Sammy Baugh was one of the first great passing quarterbacks in NFL history. Known as "Slingin' Sammy," Baugh led the NFL in passer rating six times between 1937 and 1949. The only time that mark has been matched in league history was by Hall of Famer Steve Young in the 1990s. Baugh was also one of the greatest punters in NFL history. His average of 51.40 yards per punt during the 1940 season is still the highest in NFL history.

19 JOHNNY UNITAS

Jersey number: 19
Years in NFL: 1956–1973
Year inducted into Hall of Fame: 1979

Johnny Unitas set the standard for modern quarterbacks while starring with the Baltimore Colts. Unitas was a legendary hero who thrived on pressure in big games and key moments. He led the NFL in touchdown passes for four straight seasons from 1957 to 1960. During that time, he set a record by throwing for touchdowns in 47 consecutive games. The record lasted 52 years before being broken by Drew Brees in 2012.

COOL *UNDER PRESSURE*

The greatest quarterbacks are at their best when the game is on the line. Joe Montana played with the San Francisco 49ers and Kansas City Chiefs between 1979 and 1994. He was so calm and collected—even when his team was trailing in the fourth quarter—that he was known as "Joe Cool." Montana led one of the greatest last-minute comeback drives in football history on January 22, 1989, in Super Bowl XXIII.

Joe Cool and his 49ers trailed the Cincinnati Bengals 16–13 with 3:20 remaining in the game and the ball on their own eight-yard line. Over the next 11 plays, Montana drove the 49ers almost the entire length of the field to score the game-winning touchdown with just 34 seconds left on the clock. The 49ers stopped the Bengals on the final four plays and won the game 20–16. It was the third of four Super Bowl wins for Montana with the 49ers.

Here's what San Francisco's Super Bowl–winning drive looked like:

8th play
Montana to Rice, pass incomplete. 1:36 remaining; 35 yards to go.

10th play
Montana completes an eight-yard pass to Craig. 39 seconds remaining; 10 yards to go.

11th play
Montana completes a touchdown pass to wide receiver John Taylor. 34 seconds remaining; 92-yard drive complete.

9th play
Montana completes a 27-yard pass to Rice. 1:17 remaining; 18 yards to go.

PENALTY after the **8**th play
A San Francisco penalty moves the ball back 10 yards. 1:22 remaining; 45 yards to go.

7th play

Montana completes a 13-yard pass to Craig. 1:49 remaining; 35 yards to go.

3rd play

Montana completes a seven-yard pass to wide receiver Jerry Rice. 2:32 remaining; 70 yards to go.

2nd play

Montana completes a seven-yard pass to tight end John Frank. 2:48 remaining; 77 yards to go.

1st play

Joe Montana completes an eight-yard pass to running back Roger Craig. 3:04 remaining; 84 yards to go.

START

The 49ers began their winning drive here. 3:20 remaining; 92 yards to go.

30 40 50 40 30 20 10

*Diagram not to scale

4th play

Montana hands off to Craig. Gain of one yard. 2:16 remaining; 69 yards to go.

30 40 50 40 30 20 10

6th play

Montana completes a 17-yard pass to Rice. 1:54 remaining; 48 yards to go.

5th play

Montana hands off to Craig. Gain of four yards. 2:00 remaining; 65 yards to go.

THE **GREATEST** OF ALL TIME?

Who's the GOAT—or Greatest of All Time—of all the quarterbacks in NFL history? Is it the QB with the best career passing statistics? Is it the QB with the most Super Bowl wins? Or is it the QB who has an impressive combination of passing numbers and championship victories? Let's take a look at the different ways you can measure the success of quarterbacks. Who do you think is the GOAT?

BART STARR

BIG NUMBERS

Dan Marino was the quarterback for the Miami Dolphins from 1983 to 1999. During those seasons, Marino set records that seemed almost impossible to believe. Many of those records have since been broken, but Marino was the first QB to pass for 5,000 yards in a single season and the first to pass for more than 50,000 yards in his career. The Dolphins were always a good team with Marino at quarterback, but they never won the Super Bowl. For most experts ranking the greatest ever, Dan Marino's lack of a Super Bowl title has always cost him.

DAN MARINO

FOOTBALL LEGENDS

Piling up big numbers is impressive, but winning championships is the ultimate goal. That's why guys like Peyton Manning, Brett Favre, John Elway, Joe Montana, Bart Starr, and Johnny Unitas usually get lots of consideration. They all had stellar statistics in their day, and they were Super Bowl champions, too.

MODERN CHAMPIONS

There are some current quarterbacks who could be contenders for the GOAT, too. Green Bay's Aaron Rodgers is a Super Bowl champ who's climbing career passing lists. Plus, he's got those passer rating records.

When it comes to big statistics and a ton of championships, it's hard to argue with Tom Brady. Since he became the starting quarterback of the New England Patriots in 2001, Brady has become one of the leading passers in NFL history. Now with Tampa Bay, he has led his teams to 10 Super Bowl appearances and has won seven championships.

TOM BRADY

Top 5 Single-Season Passer Ratings (through 2020)

PLAYER	TEAM	SEASON	RATING
Aaron Rodgers	Green Bay	2011	122.5
Aaron Rodgers	Green Bay	2020	121.5
Peyton Manning	Indianapolis	2004	121.1
Nick Foles	Philadelphia	2013	119.2
Ryan Tannehill	Tennessee	2019	117.5

STAT STORY

Norm Van Brocklin may not be the greatest quarterback of all time, but his record for most passing yards in a single game is one of the greatest in football history ... and he's held it for a really long time. Van Brocklin wasn't even supposed to play when he set the record for most passing yards in a game on the first day of the 1951 NFL season. He got to start for the Los Angeles Rams that day because his teammate Bob Waterfield was injured. Van Brocklin certainly made the most of his opportunity. He completed 27 of 41 passes for 554 yards and tossed for four touchdowns to lead the Rams to a 54–14 victory over a short-lived NFL team known as the New York Yanks.

CATCHING PASSES

When a quarterback throws the ball, he needs someone to catch it. Did you know that not everyone on a football field is allowed to receive a forward pass? Only some players are considered to be an "eligible receiver." Others are ineligible, which means they're not allowed to catch a forward pass.

Every player who lines up in the backfield behind the line of scrimmage is an eligible receiver. That means all running backs—who might be referred to as half-backs, fullbacks, tailbacks, slotbacks, or wingbacks—can receive a pass. Even the quarterback is eligible in most offensive formations.

Among the seven players on the line of scrimmage (see page 28), only the two players on either end of the line are eligible receivers. These players are usually a tight end or a wide receiver. The other five players on the line of scrimmage—the center, guards, and tackles—are all ineligible receivers, but they're still important to the passing game. Their job is to block the defensive players, keeping them away from the quarterback and giving the QB as much time as possible to find an open receiver.

All 11 players on defense in American football, and all 12 defensive players in Canadian football, are considered eligible to catch the ball. This means that even though offensive linemen aren't allowed to catch a pass, defensive linemen can make an interception.

THE FIRST WIDE RECEIVER

Although forward passing has been allowed in American football since 1906, teams in the NFL didn't pass much until the 1930s. When NFL teams began to throw the ball during a game, they often found it hard to pass to the players on the end of the line of scrimmage. That's because there weren't yet any strategies devised to spread out players wide toward the sidelines of the field. Everyone lined up tight near the ball along or behind the line of scrimmage. Because of that, the defense could play close together, too. The ends found it hard to get open for a catch with so many defensive players all around them. So, some teams began experimenting by moving one of their ends farther away toward the sidelines. More space between the players meant more room to throw the ball.

QUARTERBACK DAVEY O'BRIEN WAS AN EARLY PASSING STAR AT TEXAS CHRISTIAN UNIVERSITY.

PENCIL POWER

When quarterback Norm Van Brocklin set the single-game record of 554 yards passing for the Los Angeles Rams in 1951, eight different receivers caught passes from him. Here's a list of the receivers who caught passes in Van Brocklin's big game, along with the number of receptions each player had and the number of yards they gained in that game. Can you calculate the average yards per catch for each receiver and then rank the eight players from highest to lowest average yards?

In order to calculate the average yards per catch for a receiver, you need to divide the number of yards by the number of catches. For example, if a player caught 8 passes for 100 yards, the formula would be: yards ÷ catches. So, the average yards in this case would be **100 ÷ 8 = 12.5.**

PLAYER	RECEPTIONS	YARDS
Elroy Hirsch	9	173
Tom Fears	7	162
Verda T. Smith	2	103
Tommy Kalmanir	2	40
Dan Towler	2	30
Jerry Williams	2	22
Tom Keane	2	10
Bob Boyd	1	14

ANSWERS:
Elroy Hirsch: 173 ÷ 9 = 19.22. He ranks 4th.
Tom Fears: 162 ÷ 7 = 23.14. He ranks 2nd.
Verda T. Smith: 103 ÷ 2 = 51.5. He ranks 1st.
Tommy Kalmanir: 40 ÷ 2 = 20. He ranks 3rd.
Dan Towler: 30 ÷ 2 = 15. He ranks 5th.
Jerry Williams: 22 ÷ 2 = 11. He ranks 7th.
Tom Keane: 10 ÷ 2 = 5. He ranks 8th.
Bob Boyd: 14 ÷ 1 = 14. He ranks 6th.

STATSTARS

Although the position he played was technically called split end (he's also been referred to as a super end), Don Hutson is considered the NFL's first great wide receiver. He starred with the Green Bay Packers from 1935 to 1945. His very first catch in his first NFL game was an 83-yard touchdown. Hutson set 18 NFL records for receivers during his career, but most of them have now been broken.

Don Hutson was a great match with Packers quarterback Arnie Herber, who loved to throw the ball long. Herber was the first quarterback to pass for over 1,000 yards in a season when he threw for 1,239 yards in 1936. Hutson became the first receiver to top 1,000 yards, catching 72 passes for 1,211 yards in 1942. These days, the best quarterbacks might pass for over 5,000 yards in a season, but anything over 1,000 yards is still considered a great number for any receiver.

TOM FEARS OF THE LOS ANGELES RAMS

PASS PATTERNS

Right angles, acute angles, obtuse angles, degrees—it's all math, or, more specifically, geometry. But what does this have to do with football? You may be surprised to learn just how much geometry is involved in running pass patterns.

A great pass receiver needs strong hands. It helps to be fast, too. It also doesn't hurt to throw in a few fake moves to make the defense think you're going the other way. But even receivers who aren't very speedy or shifty can be effective if they can run precise patterns. That means making their cuts at the proper angle—and angles are what geometry is all about. Check out these basic pass patterns with various angles.

PASS RECEIVERS BEGINNING THEIR PATTERNS

OUT

Sometimes known as a down and out or a square-out. The receiver runs straight for a fixed distance, usually 10 yards, and then makes a sharp 90-degree cut to "the outside" toward the sidelines.

IN

Sometimes known as a down and in or a dig route. The receiver runs straight for a fixed distance, usually 10 yards, and then makes a sharp 90-degree cut to "the inside" toward the middle of the field.

POST

Post routes are used for longer pass plays. The receiver runs straight for about 10 or 20 yards, then cuts at a 45-degree angle into the middle of the field and runs toward the goal posts. That's how this route got its name.

CORNER

Sometimes known as a flag. This is a similar route to the post but in a different direction. The receiver runs straight for about 10 or 20 yards, then cuts at a 45-degree angle toward the corner of the end zone and runs toward the flags there.

HOOK

Sometimes known as a hitch or a button hook. This is a short pass play. The receiver runs straight for 10 yards or less and then abruptly stops and turns to run back toward the quarterback. The ball should arrive almost as soon as the receiver has made his turn.

BATTLING FOR A CATCH

FLY

Sometimes called a streak route or a go route. The receiver runs straight up the field toward the other team's end zone. There are no cuts or angles in this route. Passes like these are sometimes referred to as bombs or long bombs. Late in a game, a team might send three or five receivers to run a fly route, hoping to get a lucky catch. When they do that, the play is often known as a Hail Mary pass.

ROUTE TREE

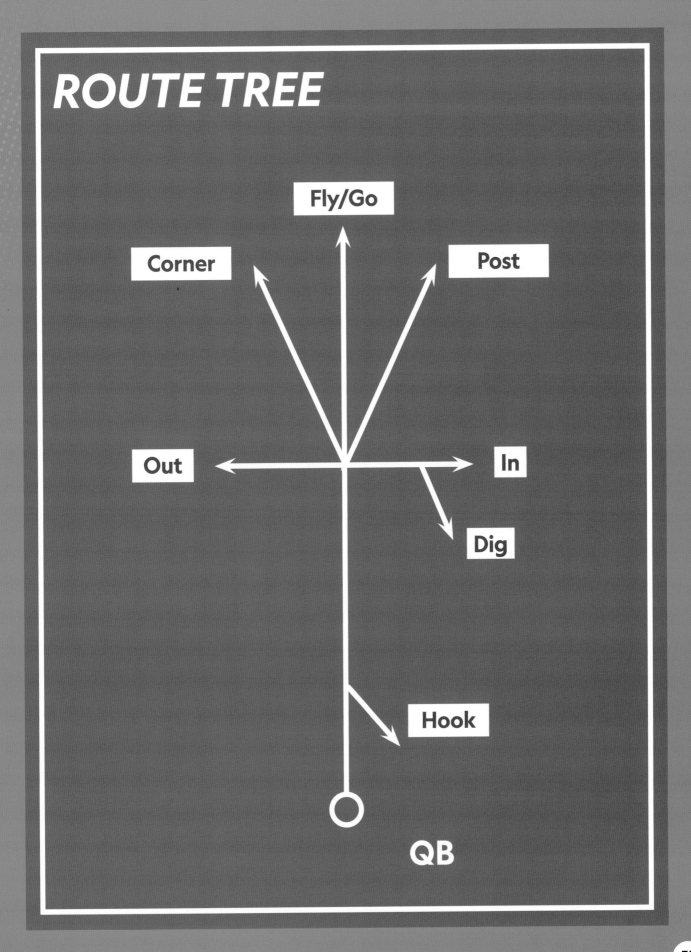

WHO WORE WHAT NUMBER:
RECEIVERS

If you catch enough passes, and come up big in clutch situations, the fans in the stands might chant your name in celebration. Do it often enough for long enough, and you're likely to wind up in the Hall of Fame when your career is over, just like these stars of the NFL and CFL.

BOB HAYES

12

Jersey number: 12
Position: Wide receiver
Years in NFL: 1965–1975
Year inducted into Hall of Fame: 2009

Bob Hayes made his NFL debut with the Dallas Cowboys in 1965. A year earlier, he won gold medals in the 100 meters and the 4 × 100 relay at the 1964 Summer Olympics. Hayes is the only athlete to win an Olympic gold medal and a Super Bowl ring, which he won with Dallas in Super Bowl VI. He led the Cowboys in catches three times.

ELROY HIRSCH

40

Jersey number: 40
Position: Wide receiver
Years in NFL: 1946–1957
Year inducted into Hall of Fame: 1968

Elroy Hirsch was called "Crazy Legs" because of the unusual way his legs twisted when he ran. His style didn't seem to slow him down. He was a halfback who became a wide receiver, and with his sprinter speed he became football's first true "deep threat." That means long, fast running catches were his specialty. When Hirsch led the NFL with 17 touchdowns in 1951, 10 of them came on long bombs.

BILL HEWITT

56

Jersey number: 56
Position: End
Years in NFL: 1932–1939; 1943
Year inducted into Hall of Fame: 1971

In the early days, before football players specialized in offense or defense, Bill Hewitt was a star end on both the offensive line and the defensive line. On offense, he was credited with inventing many trick plays, including catching a pass and then making a lateral pass to his team's other end. Hewitt was the first player to be named All-NFL (a league all-star) for two different teams: 1933, 1934, and 1936 with the Chicago Bears and 1937 with the Philadelphia Eagles.

80 JERRY RICE

Jersey number: 80
Position: Wide receiver
Years in NFL: 1985–2004
Year inducted into Hall of Fame: 2010

Jerry Rice is the NFL's all-time leader with 1,549 catches and 22,895 receiving yards. He also holds the record for the most seasons with 1,000 or more receiving yards (14), the most games with 100 or more receiving yards (76), and the most consecutive games with a pass reception (274). Rice set numerous Super Bowl records with the San Francisco 49ers, including most career touchdowns (8), most career catches (33), and most career yardage (589). With all those records, Rice really was a San Francisco treat.

84 SHANNON SHARPE

Jersey number: 84
Position: Tight end
Years in NFL: 1990–2003
Year inducted into Hall of Fame: 2011

When he retired in 2003, Shannon Sharpe was the all-time leader among tight ends with 815 catches, 10,060 receiving yards, and 62 touchdowns. Those records have since been broken, but Sharpe won the Super Bowl twice with the Denver Broncos and once with the Baltimore Ravens. He was selected to the Pro Bowl (all-star game) eight times.

77 TONY GABRIEL

Jersey number: 77
Position: Tight end
Years in CFL: 1971–1981
Year inducted into Hall of Fame: 1985

Tony Gabriel was an outstanding tight end in the CFL for 11 seasons. He topped 1,000 receiving yards five times in his career. Gabriel was named the CFL's Most Outstanding Canadian in 1974, 1976, 1977, and 1978 and the league's Most Outstanding Player in 1978. Always a strong player when the game was on the line, Gabriel's three last-minute catches helped the Hamilton Tiger-Cats win the Grey Cup championship in 1972. And he caught the winning touchdown pass with 20 seconds left in the game to give the Ottawa Rough Riders the Grey Cup in 1976.

88 LYNN SWANN

Jersey number: 88
Position: Wide receiver
Years in NFL: 1974–1982
Year inducted into Hall of Fame: 2001

Lynn Swann had graceful moves and tremendous leaping ability, which allowed him to make many highlight-reel catches. Swann moved with grace on the football field. In fact, he had studied many forms of dance, including ballet, from the age of four until his final year of high school. Swann was the MVP of Super Bowl X when his Pittsburgh Steelers defeated the Dallas Cowboys.

TRY THIS!

Make the Play

You've learned all about some of the best quarterbacks and receivers in football history—what they do on the field and how to calculate their statistics. You've also read about some of the pass patterns used by quarterbacks and receivers. Now it's time to see what kind of plays you can create.

Think about the angles of the patterns described on previous pages and see if you can come up with your own patterns. Consider some zigzags or combining different cuts with several different angles. Sketch them out on a few pieces of paper first. You can even come up with names for your plays. It could be something as simple as a description of the moves you want done. For example, an out pattern with an extra 90-degree cut upfield could be an "out and up" or a "down out and down." You can get more creative, too. A zigzag move could be called a "lightning bolt," or a play designed for a specific friend to run, like your buddy Teddy, could have his or her name or nickname used as the name of the play—the Teddy Bear!

When you're ready, find yourself a football, a friend, and a field. Then test out your pass patterns. (Don't forget to ask permission from an adult before you head out!) You're probably not as good a quarterback as Tom Brady— yet—and your plays might not actually work in an NFL game, but if you can get your geometry right, you might score some touchdowns!

PLAY BOOK

Isaak—WR Sam—WR Eli—TE Miles—RB Teddy—QB

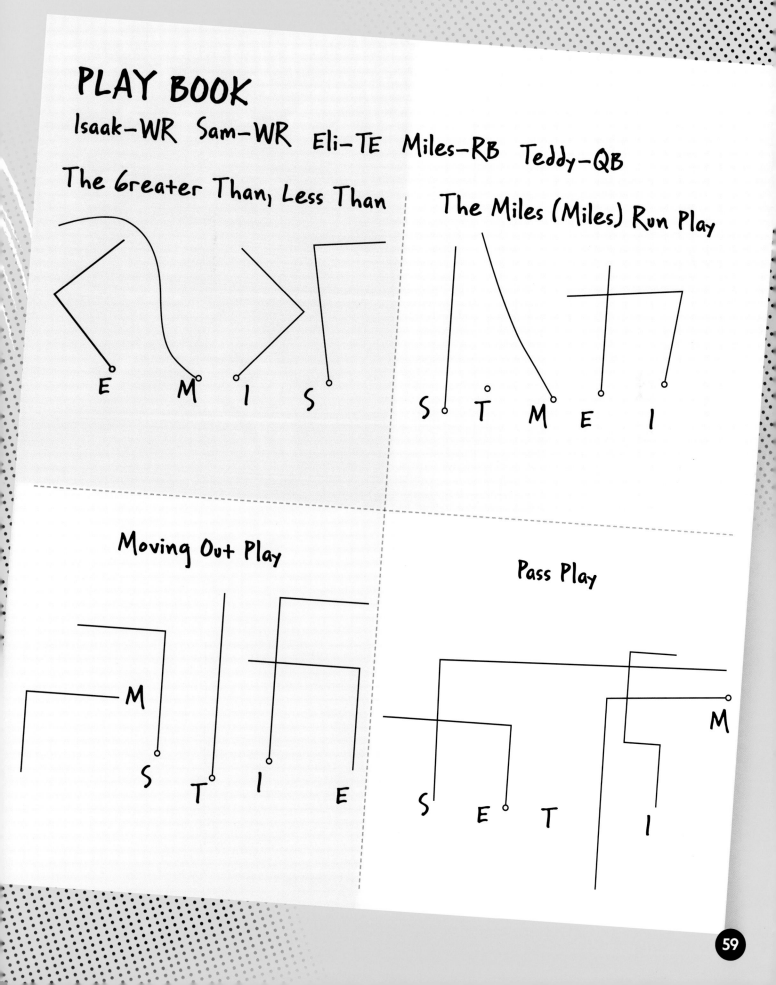

The Greater Than, Less Than

E M I S

The Miles (Miles) Run Play

S T M E I

Moving Out Play

S T I E

Pass Play

S E T I M

CHAPTER FOUR

THE RUNNING

GAME

There's a lot of running in football. A quarterback can scramble in the backfield, or a defensive player might have to chase down the ballcarrier to tackle him. But none of this is what people mean when they talk about the running game. The running game is when a running back takes the ball from the quarterback and, well ... runs with it.

The NFL record book officially credits anyone who runs with the ball on a running play with an attempt (like a pass attempt). Even so, people usually call it a carry, as in the player carries the ball. And just to put one more term on the table: Yards gained on these running plays are usually referred to as rushing yards, not running yards.

STATSTARS

In more than 100 years of NFL history, there have only been seven times when two players on the same team rushed (or ran) for 1,000 yards or more in the same season:

1972 Miami Dolphins	Larry Csonka – 1,117	Mercury Morris – 1,000
1976 Pittsburgh Steelers	Franco Harris – 1,128	Rocky Bleier – 1,036
1985 Cleveland Browns	Kevin Mack – 1,104	Earnest Byner – 1,002
2006 Atlanta Falcons	Warrick Dunn – 1,140	Michael Vick – 1,039
2008 New York Giants	Brandon Jacobs – 1,089	Derrick Ward – 1,025
2009 Carolina Panthers	Jonathan Stewart – 1,113	DeAngelo Williams – 1,117
2019 Baltimore Ravens	Lamar Jackson – 1,206	Mark Ingram II – 1,018

STRENGTH AND SPEED

Strength and speed are very important in football. The fastest players are usually wide receivers, cornerbacks, and running backs. A good blocker on the offensive line needs strength more than speed, but they also need science. It turns out that running backs require a lot of science, too. Grab your lab coat, and let's go all STEM on this game.

THE STUDY OF MOTION

When talking about motion in football, we look at three key points: position, speed, and acceleration. Position can be as simple as where a running back lines up on the field. They line up in the backfield, usually a few steps away from the quarterback and even farther away from the defensive line. A running back will usually have a few steps to accelerate, or speed up, before a defensive player can get to him. The runner hopes to achieve a high speed as quickly as he can.

Some running backs don't have a lot of speed, but they can accelerate quickly. This gives them a burst of speed to pull away from the defense until someone faster catches up and tackles them. Other runners are slow to accelerate, but once they do, they can reach a high speed.

Sometimes a running back will start out slowly on purpose. The runner might move carefully, to the right or left, waiting for an opening in the offensive line. When he sees it, he has to accelerate quickly. He plants a foot down hard onto the field. The force he applies stops his sideways motion and allows him to accelerate forward. If he can accelerate quickly, he will start to gain speed. Even though the running back may be faster than the defensive players, if the defenders can accelerate more quickly, they'll tackle him before he can speed away.

THE NEED FOR SPEED

When top college football players are being scouted for the NFL, one of the tests they're put through is running a 40-yard dash, which is a great way to measure, or time, their speed. The current NFL record for running the 40-yard dash was set in 2017 by wide receiver John Ross before he was drafted by the Cincinnati Bengals. Ross covered the distance in 4.22 seconds.

MONTEZ SWEAT RUNS THE 40.

SCIENCE STUFF

In the late 1600s, Sir Isaac Newton helped revolutionize science with his three laws of motion to describe the physical world. Newton probably didn't have football in mind, but there's an awful lot of physics involved in making a good block.

Blocking is as simple as one player trying to stop another player from advancing. To do that, one body has to exert a certain amount of force on another body. Newton's third law of motion says that when two bodies collide, each body exerts a force on the other that is equal but in the opposite direction. In order for one lineman to be able to push another out of the way, it helps to have a lower center of mass. That just means keeping your body low and driving up into your opponent's body. This will throw off your opponent's center of mass and allow you to use more torque (rotational force) to push him in the direction you need him to go.

STAT STORY

Since 2016, the NFL has been using radar to track the fastest speed a player reaches in miles per hour (MPH) on any given play. In 2019, the maximum speed for an NFL player was 22.3 miles per hour by running back Matt Breida of the San Francisco 49ers. He hit that high during an 83-yard touchdown run against the Cleveland Browns in week five of the season. Breida also had the fastest speed (22.09 MPH) in 2018, making him the first player to top the NFL in MPH two years in a row.

CAM NEWTON'S ACCELERATION AND AGILITY HELP HIM AVOID A TACKLE.

RECORD RUNNERS

It's rare that a football weekend goes by without a handful of running backs rushing over 100 yards in a game. The last time the NFL played a full season without at least one running back rushing for over 1,000 yards was all the way back in 1969. A 100-yard game and a 1,000-yard season are milestones for any running back. Let's take a look at those and some of the other important running records.

FIRST AND LONG

As a rookie with the Chicago Bears in 1934, Beattie Feathers became the first player in NFL history to rush for 1,000 yards. Although an injury kept him out of the last two games of the season, Feathers gained 1,004 yards on just 119 carries in the 11 games he played.

Feathers's average of 8.44 yards per carry in 1934 remained an NFL record for 72 years before it was finally broken in 2006. That year, Michael Vick of the Atlanta Falcons became the first quarterback to rush for 1,000 yards. He gained 1,039 yards on only 123 carries to edge Feathers out of the top spot with an average of 8.45 yards per carry. Among running backs, Feathers is still the record holder today.

BEATTIE FEATHERS (LEFT) RUNS BEHIND BEARS TEAMMATE BRONKO NAGURSKI.

BIG GAME PLAYER

Marion Motley was a star with the Cleveland Browns at two different positions from 1946 to 1953. He played linebacker on defense and fullback on offense. His rushing statistics don't look all that impressive to modern eyes, yet some of Motley's numbers are truly amazing.

Motley enjoyed the best game of his career on October 29, 1950. The Browns beat the Pittsburgh Steelers 45–7. Motley rushed for 188 yards that day. He did it on just 11 carries. That makes his average of 17.09 yards per carry the highest ever in a single game for any running back or fullback with at least 10 carries.

STATSTARS

Emmitt Smith holds the NFL career record with 18,355 yards rushing. He also holds the record for most career carries with 4,409. And he's the all-time leader for most 1,000-yard rushing seasons with 11, which he did 11 years in a row with the Dallas Cowboys from 1991 to 2001. Smith had 78 career games in which he topped 100 yards rushing, which is just ahead of Walter Payton (77) and Barry Sanders (76). Smith holds yet another NFL record with his 164 career rushing touchdowns.

PENCIL POWER

To figure out a player's average yards per carry, divide the number of yards by the number of carries. **Here's the formula:**

Number of yards ÷ Number of carries = Average yards per carry

For example, for Beattie Feathers, that's 1,004 yards divided by 119 carries:

1,004 ÷ 119 = 8.4369747. This rounds off to 8.44.

Can you figure out the average yards per carry for these rushing leaders?

Emmitt Smith's career record: 18,355 yards on 4,409 carries.

Eric Dickerson's 1984 single season record: 2,105 yards on 404 carries

ERIC DICKERSON

ANSWER:
Emmitt Smith: 18,355 ÷ 4,409 = 4.16 yards per carry
Eric Dickerson: 2,105 ÷ 404 = 5.21 yards per carry

RUNNING PLAYS

Just like a quarterback needs the offensive line for protection on passing plays, even the fastest or shiftiest running back won't get far without good blockers. On running plays, the center, two guards, and two offensive tackles push forward against the defensive line, blocking for the running backs by opening up spaces between defensive players. These spaces are known as holes, and these holes are the key to most running plays.

DEFOREST BUCKNER BLOCKED BY PATRICK MEKARI

NUMBERING THE BACKFIELD:

When coaches draw up plays for the offense, they simplify things by using numbers and letters to represent the players who might get the ball. It looks like some sort of code, but with the key, you, too, can decipher the message.

1 = Quarterback
2 = Primary running back
3 = Fullback
4 = Secondary running back

Y = Tight end
X = Wide receiver
Z = Other receiver

Also, in the charts to the right, don't forget the abbreviations we learned early for the players on the offensive line:

C = Center
LG/RG = Left guard/Right guard
LT/RT = Left tackle/Right tackle

HOLE NUMBERS

Offensive linemen don't get numbers to represent them on plays, but the holes—the spaces between them—do. Each hole on the offensive line has its own number.

In most offensive schemes, the holes on the left side of the center are given odd numbers. The holes on the right side have even numbers. It works like this:

| | LT | LG | C | RG | RT | |
| 5 | 3 | 1 | 2 | 4 | 6 |

If a tight end plays on the left side, there's a 7 hole around that end of the line:

| Y | | LT | LG | C | RG | RT |
| 7 | 5 | 3 | 1 | 2 | 4 | 6 |

If a tight is on the right, there's an 8 hole around the right end of the line:

| | LT | LG | C | RG | RT | Y |
| 5 | 3 | 1 | 2 | 4 | 6 | 8 |

Sometimes, the area directly through center is labeled as the 0 hole:

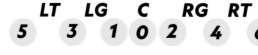

| | LT | LG | C | | RG | RT | |
| 5 | 3 | 1 | 0 | 2 | 4 | 6 |

CALLING PLAYS

If a coach wants the primary running back to take the ball from the quarterback and run through the hole between the right guard and the right tackle, the play would be labeled 24. That's 2 for the running back and 4 for the hole. If the fullback is supposed to run between the left tackle and the tight end on the left, that would be a 35. The first number is always the ball carrier, while the second number is always the hole.

Plays often have a descriptive term added to the number. For example, a 24-Dive would be a play where the running back takes the ball from the quarterback and plunges directly through the hole between the right guard and the right tackle. A dive is usually a short yardage play. 24-Lead means the fullback goes through the 4 hole first, providing a lead blocker for the running back.

A play where the ball carrier runs around the end of the line is usually known as a sweep. A 27-Sweep would send the primary running back around the left end of the line. A 38-Sweep would send the fullback around the right side.

Coaches can make things as tricky as they'd like. On a 17-X Reverse, the quarterback would start running around the hole beyond the tight end on the left side. Instead of continuing the sweep, he would give the ball to the wide receiver (X), who would run in the reverse direction.

TAMPA BAY HEAD COACH
BRUCE ARIANS CALLING PLAYS
FROM THE GAME PLAN

These Hall of Fame running backs were among the best in football throughout the years.

27 MIKE PRINGLE

Jersey number: 27
Years in the CFL: 1992–2004
Year inducted into Hall of Fame: 2008

Mike Pringle played 13 seasons in the CFL with four different teams but mainly with the Montreal Alouettes from 1996 to 2002. Pringle led the CFL in rushing six times. He set a league record with 1,972 yards in 1994, and then broke it with 2,065 yards in 1998. In his final season, Pringle broke George Reed's career record of 16,116 yards and finished his own career with 16,425. He was named the CFL's Most Outstanding Player twice and his teams won the Grey Cup two times.

32 MARCUS ALLEN

Jersey number: 32
Years in NFL: 1982–1997
Year inducted into Hall of Fame: 2003

Marcus Allen was the first running back in NFL history to rush for more than 10,000 yards and to catch passes for more than 5,000 yards. Allen burst onto the scene in his early days, winning the Heisman Trophy as the best player in the NCAA in 1981 and then being named the Offensive Rookie of the Year with the Los Angeles Raiders in 1982. At the end of the following season, he was named the MVP of the Super Bowl.

34 EARL CAMPBELL

Jersey number: 34
Years in NFL: 1978–1985
Year inducted into Hall of Fame: 1991

In his first season with the Houston Oilers, Earl Campbell led the NFL in rushing and was named the Offensive Rookie of the Year and the league MVP. He was the rushing leader for the next two seasons as well. Campbell just missed becoming the second player to rush for 2,000 yards with 1,934 in 1980. He did set a record that still stands by rushing for 200 or more yards in four games that season.

JEROME BETTIS

36

Jersey number: 36
Years in NFL: 1993–2005
Year inducted into Hall of Fame: 2015

Standing just 5'11" (1.8 m), but weighing 252 pounds (114.3 kg), Jerome Bettis was incredibly strong. He became known as "The Bus" because he could carry players on his back when they tried to tackle him. In his first season with the Los Angeles Rams, Bettis became the eighth rookie in NFL history with a 200-yard game. He had the first of his eight 1,000-yard rushing seasons that year (six of them with the Pittsburgh Steelers), which was tied for third in NFL history at the time of his retirement.

GALE SAYERS

40

Jersey number: 40
Years in NFL: 1965–1971
Year inducted into Hall of Fame: 1977

Gale Sayers played four full seasons with the Chicago Bears and only parts of three other seasons because of injuries. When he was healthy, he could make moves on the football field like nobody had ever seen. In 1965, Sayers set rookie records with 22 touchdowns and 132 points. On December 12, 1965, he tied an all-time record with six touchdowns.

RED GRANGE

77

Jersey number: 77
Years in NFL: 1925–1934
Year inducted into Hall of Fame: 1963

Known as the "Galloping Ghost," Red Grange was a national hero at the University of Illinois in the early 1920s. College stars rarely turned pro in those days, but Grange gave the NFL instant credibility when he joined the Chicago Bears on Thanksgiving Day in 1925. Grange played five league games and several more exhibition games. It's believed he was paid $100,000 that year at a time when most pro players were lucky to get $100 a game.

THE RUNNING OF **THE GOATS**

When it comes to determining the greatest running backs in NFL history, rushing statistics are usually considered the most important thing to look at. Let's look at the all-time rushing leaders in NFL history (through the 2020 season)—plus one player whose records have mostly been broken but who still may be the greatest of all time.

FRANK GORE

RUSHING YARDS: CAREER

Emmitt Smith (1990–2004)	18,355
Walter Payton (1975–1987)	16,726
Frank Gore (2005–2020)	16,000
Barry Sanders (1989–1998)	15,269
Adrian Peterson (2007–2020)	14,820

RUSHING YARDS: SEASON

Eric Dickerson (Los Angeles Rams, 1984)	2,105
Adrian Peterson (Minnesota Vikings, 2012)	2,097
Jamal Lewis (Baltimore Ravens, 2003)	2,066
Barry Sanders (Detroit Lions, 1997)	2,053
Derrick Henry (Tennessee Titans, 2020)	2,027

RUSHING YARDS: GAME

Adrian Peterson (Minnesota Vikings, 2007)	296
Jamal Lewis (Baltimore Ravens, 2003)	295
Jerome Harrison (Cleveland Browns, 2009)	286
Corey Dillon (Cincinnati Bengals, 2000)	278
Walter Payton (Chicago Bears, 1977)	275

ERIC DICKERSON

JEROME HARRISON

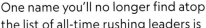

IS BROWN THE BEST?

One name you'll no longer find atop the list of all-time rushing leaders is Jim Brown. Still, many people consider him to be the greatest running back of all time. He was a first-round draft pick of the Cleveland Browns in 1957 and led the NFL in rushing yards and touchdowns that season. In just the ninth game of his career, Brown rushed for 237 yards, setting a new NFL record that would last for 14 years and a rookie record that would last for 40 years.

During his nine NFL seasons, Brown led the league in rushing eight times, which is still the all-time record. His streak of five straight rushing titles from 1957 to 1961 is also a record, and his three straight titles from 1963 to 1965 have him tied with three other players for the second longest streak in history. When he retired in 1965, Jim Brown was the NFL's all-time career leader in rushing yards (12,312), rushing touchdowns (106), and total touchdowns (126). Those records have all been broken, but to this day, Brown remains the only player in NFL history to average more than 100 yards rushing per game for his entire career.

STATSTARS

For the first two games of the 1997 season, Barry Sanders, star running back for the Detroit Lions, rushed for just 33 and 20 yards. Never before in his great career had Sanders tallied so few yards in two consecutive games. The next game, Sanders exploded for 161 yards. It was the start of an amazing streak. During each of the final 14 games of the season, Sanders topped 100 yards. His record for most consecutive 100-yard rushing games may never be broken.

TRY *THIS!*

On Your Mark, Get Set, Dash!

Let's pretend that you're a senior in college and NFL scouts for your favorite team are looking to recruit you. They'll want to see how fast you can run the 40-yard dash. So, pick a friend or two, get permission from an adult, and head out to a local field. It doesn't have to be a real football field with yardage lines—although that would help—but you will need a space large enough to measure out 40 yards. The easiest way to do this is to count 40 long steps or paces. Make sure you mark a starting spot and a finish line. If you have cones, use them as markers; otherwise a sweatshirt, a rag, or something soft (so you won't get hurt) will do.

WHAT YOU NEED:

- 2 cones (T-shirts or rags also work)
- A stopwatch or another way to time in seconds
- A pen or pencil
- Paper

1 Place your first cone.

2 Step 40 paces ahead.

3 Set down your second cone.

4 Stand near the end point with the timer.

5 Have your friend stand at the starting point. As soon as you push the start button on your timer, yell "Go!"

6 When your friend crosses the end point, push stop on the timer.

7 Write down how fast the runner went.

8 Take turns running.

Now you know how fast you can run the 40-yard dash, but what is that in miles per hour? There's a simple way to estimate that. Just take the number 80 and divide it by your time to find your miles per hour (80 ÷ your time in seconds). What did you get? What about your friend? Run this distance three times, with some breaks in between, and then find your average speed by adding up all of the times and dividing that total number by the number of times you ran the distance. Now what is it in miles per hour?

CHAPTER FIVE

DEFENSE AND SPECIAL TEAMS

Legendary NCAA football coach Paul "Bear" Bryant is known for saying, "Offense sells tickets, but defense wins championships." Coach Bryant was likely trying to say that offense might be fun, flashy, and exciting to watch, but a steady and predictable defense is the true foundation of a winning team. After all, the main role of the defense is to try and stop the offense from scoring ... and if a team doesn't score, it can't win.

In this chapter, we won't just look at the D (that's defense), we'll also look at special teams. Those are the players who are on the field for the kicking game. Special teams aren't considered defense or offense since they're usually on the field when the ball changes hands from one team to the other. Many of the players involved on the special teams, especially the kickers, tend to specialize in, or focus on, one particular skill.

DIGIT-YOU-KNOW?

Great defensive teams are measured by how few yards or points they allow. These teams have had the NFL's best defensive statistics the most times:

MOST SEASONS LEADING THE LEAGUE, FEWEST POINTS ALLOWED

12 – CHICAGO BEARS
1932, 1936, 1937, 1942, 1948, 1963, 1985, 1986, 1988, 2001, 2005, 2018

MOST SEASONS LEADING THE LEAGUE, FEWEST OVERALL YARDS ALLOWED

10 – PITTSBURGH STEELERS
1957, 1974, 1976, 1990, 2001, 2004, 2007, 2008, 2011, 2012

MOST SEASONS LEADING THE LEAGUE, FEWEST RUSHING YARDS ALLOWED

11 – CHICAGO BEARS
1937, 1939, 1942, 1946, 1949, 1963, 1984, 1985, 1987, 1988, 2018

MOST SEASONS LEADING THE LEAGUE, FEWEST PASSING YARDS ALLOWED

10 – GREEN BAY PACKERS
1947, 1948, 1962, 1964, 1965, 1966, 1967, 1968, 1996, 2005

DEFENSIVE STATISTICS

Individually, defensive players can be measured by their own unique statistics, such as:

Tackles: taking down the ballcarrier
Sacks: tackling the quarterback behind the line of scrimmage
Interceptions: catching passes intended for offensive players
Fumble recoveries: picking up the ball when an offensive player drops it

Here's a look at the players who hold the records in these four key defensive statistics for a game, a season, or an entire career.

LUKE KUECHLY MAKES A TACKLE.

TACKLES

MOST IN A GAME:

24 LUKE KUECHLY (CAROLINA PANTHERS, 2013)
DAVID HARRIS (NEW YORK JETS, 2007)

2,059 MOST IN A CAREER:
RAY LEWIS (BALTIMORE RAVENS, 1996–2012)

STATSTARS

Deacon Jones is considered to be one of the greatest defensive ends of all time. He's also the man who came up with the term "sack" to describe tackling the quarterback behind the line of scrimmage on a passing play. The idea came from an ancient military term used when an army destroyed a rival city.

Jones retired in 1974, and the NFL didn't begin to officially track sacks until 1982. If it had done so when Jones was playing, his 26 sacks in a 14-game season in 1967, and the 173.5 sacks he had in his 13-year career, would still rank among the all-time leaders.

SACKS

MOST IN A GAME:
7.0 DERRICK THOMAS
(KANSAS CITY CHIEFS, 1990)

DERRICK THOMAS SACKS STEVE YOUNG.

MOST IN A CAREER:
200 BRUCE SMITH
(BUFFALO BILLS, WASHINGTON, 1985–2003)

BRUCE SMITH SACKS STEVE MCNAIR.

DIGIT-YOU-KNOW?
Any time that multiple defensive players combine on a play to sack the quarterback, each player contributing to the sack is credited with half a sack, even if there were more than two players involved.

DEFENSIVE FUMBLE RECOVERIES

MOST IN A GAME:
3 SHARED BY 15 PLAYERS

INTERCEPTIONS

MOST IN A GAME:
4 SHARED BY 19 PLAYERS

MOST IN A SEASON:
9 DON HULTZ
(MINNESOTA VIKINGS, 1963)

MOST IN A SEASON:
14 DICK "NIGHT TRAIN" LANE
(LOS ANGELES RAMS, 1952)

MOST IN A CAREER:
81 PAUL KRAUSE
(WASHINGTON, MINNESOTA VIKINGS, 1964–1979)

MOST IN A CAREER:
29 JIM MARSHALL
(CLEVELAND BROWNS, MINNESOTA VIKINGS, 1960–1979)
JASON TAYLOR (MIAMI DOLPHINS, WASHINGTON, NEW YORK JETS, 1997–2011)

DEFENSIVE FORMATIONS

Defensive formations are the different ways that coaches line up their players on defense. Some of these formations are better for trying to stop the offense from passing. Others are better at trying to shut down the running game. The numbers used to describe defensive formations refer to the defensive linemen and the linebackers who play behind them. The first number always represents the linemen, and the second number represents the linebackers. The secondary, or defensive backs—the cornerbacks and safeties—get left out of these numbers. These are the most common defensive formations in American football:

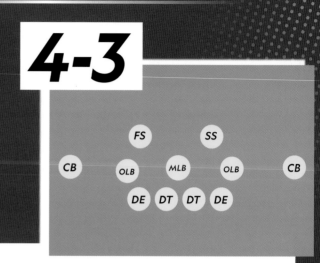

4-3

FOUR DEFENSIVE LINEMEN AND THREE LINEBACKERS

This is the most commonly used defense at the highest levels of football. The number 4 represents the four linemen on the line of scrimmage—two tackles and two ends. Behind them are three linebackers, and then two safeties and two cornerbacks forming the secondary. This is the most versatile defense for stopping the running game and the passing game.

3-4

THREE DEFENSIVE LINEMEN AND FOUR LINEBACKERS

Playing a team that likes to use short passes? Try this setup. There are only three defensive linemen on the line of scrimmage and four linebackers. Often, one of the four linebackers will have extra pass coverage responsibilities along with the four players in the secondary. With five players focusing on passing duties, the 3-4 defense is sometimes known as the "nickel" defense.

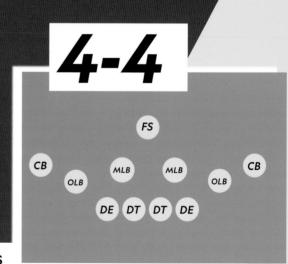

4-4

FOUR DEFENSIVE LINEMEN AND FOUR LINEBACKERS

Sometimes known as a "stack" defense, this formation features four linemen, four linebackers, and only three players in the secondary: two cornerbacks and one safety. It's good for defending against teams that like to run toward the sidelines or use short passes. It's often used when a defensive team is going to blitz, which is a pass rush (pressuring a quarterback when he's trying to throw) using a lot of players—often four or more.

5-2

FIVE DEFENSIVE LINEMEN AND TWO LINEBACKERS

If you watch a lot of high school or college football, you've probably seen this popular defense. It's mainly used against the run but is also good for pressuring the quarterback on passing plays. The five players on the line of scrimmage include a nose guard/nose tackle in the center flanked by two tackles and two ends. There are only two linebackers, plus four players in the secondary.

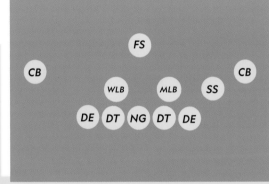

5-3

FIVE DEFENSIVE LINEMEN AND THREE LINEBACKERS

This defense is even more focused on stopping the run. It includes the same five players on the line of scrimmage as in the 5–2, but there are three linebackers instead of two and only three players in the secondary instead of four.

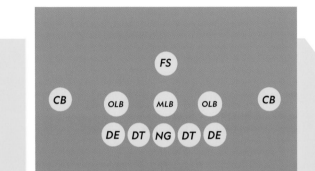

6-2

SIX DEFENSIVE LINEMEN AND TWO LINEBACKERS

In this formation, there are two nose guards/nose tackles along with two tackles and two ends on the line of scrimmage. Only two linebackers and three players are in the secondary. This is often used as a short-yard defense when the offense is close to a first down or a touchdown.

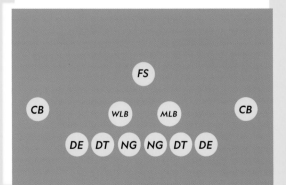

DEFENSIVE NICKNAMES

Sometimes numbers are not enough. These defensive players—sometimes the whole defensive team—were so strong that people knew them by name. Well, not necessarily the individual names of the players ... these entire teams had their own nicknames!

ORANGE CRUSH

Inspired by the bright orange jerseys they wore at home and a popular brand of soda, a *Denver Post* columnist came up with this name for the Broncos defense of the 1970s. Denver's 3-4 defense was anchored by lineman Lyle Alzado and linebackers Tom Jackson and Randy Gradishar. They led the Broncos to their first Super Bowl appearance in 1978 in Super Bowl XII.

PURPLE PEOPLE EATERS

Another colorful 1970s nickname was inspired by the purple jerseys of the home team and a popular song of the 1950s. This Minnesota Vikings unit featured a front four of offensive linemen Alan Page, Carl Eller, Jim Marshall, and Gary Larsen. Minnesota reached the Super Bowl four times in the 1970s but never won it.

NO-NAME DEFENSE

This nickname began as an insult when Dallas coach Tom Landry said he couldn't remember the names of the Miami defensive players after the Cowboys crushed the Dolphins in Super Bowl VI in 1972. Miami may not have had any big-name stars on its defense, but they were good enough to lead the Dolphins to a perfect record (17-0) the next season and two straight Super Bowl titles. During the 1972 season, the Dolphins allowed an NFL-low 3,297 yards gained by other teams and a league-low 171 points scored by their opponents.

DOOMSDAY DEFENSE

The Dallas defense of the 1960s and '70s was known as the Doomsday Defense because they spelled doom for opposing offenses. The Cowboys reached the Super Bowl five times in the 1970s, more than any other team. They won it twice, including Super Bowl XII in 1978 when defensive linemen Randy White and Harvey Martin became the only co-MVPs in Super Bowl history.

STEEL CURTAIN

The Pittsburgh Steelers were four for four when it came to Super Bowl wins in the 1970s. They were led by a talented offense and a tough defense known as the Steel Curtain. The nickname was originally given to Pittsburgh's front four defensive linemen L. C. Greenwood, Ernie Holmes, Dwight White, and "Mean" Joe Greene, but it came to represent the entire Steelers defense.

FEARSOME FOURSOME

Although other teams had used it before, the nickname of the Fearsome Foursome became synonymous with the defensive line of the Los Angeles Rams of the 1960s. Deacon Jones, Merlin Olsen, Rosey Grier, and Lamar Lundy helped transform the Rams from perennial losers into an NFL powerhouse—although they never reached an NFL championship game or Super Bowl in that era.

WHO WORE WHAT NUMBER:
DEFENSIVE GOATS

hese NFL players are all in the Pro Football Hall of Fame and are usually among the names that come up when people discuss the greatest defensive players of all time. The CFL Hall of Famer here is one of Canada's all-time great defenders, too.

42 RONNIE LOTT
Jersey number: 42
Position: Cornerback/Safety
Years in NFL: 1981–1994
Year inducted into Hall of Fame: 2000

Ronnie Lott earned All-Pro (best player) honors at three different positions: cornerback, free safety, and strong safety. A hard-hitting player, Lott recorded 100 tackles or more five times in his career and led the NFL in interceptions twice. He helped the San Francisco 49ers win eight division titles and was one of only five players who were on all four of San Francisco's Super Bowl–winning teams in the 1980s.

51 DICK BUTKUS
Jersey number: 51
Position: Linebacker
Years in NFL: 1965–1973
Year inducted into Hall of Fame: 1979

Dick Butkus had the speed and agility to make tackles from sideline to sideline and to cover the best tight ends and running backs on pass plays. He had an intensity that made him look mean, but he played a clean game. Butkus was adept at forcing fumbles and recovered 25 in his career. He also had 22 interceptions.

55 WAYNE HARRIS
Jersey number: 55
Position: Defensive end
Years in CFL: 1961–1972
Year inducted into Hall of Fame: 1976

Wayne Harris played 12 seasons in the CFL, all with the Calgary Stampeders. He won the Most Outstanding Lineman Award a record four times. Harris was a West Division All-Star 11 times in his career and an overall CFL All-Star eight times. He played in the Grey Cup championship game three times, and his team won it in 1971. Harris was known as the "Thumper" because of his bone-jarring hits.

JOE GREENE

75

Jersey number: 75
Position: Defensive tackle
Years in NFL: 1969–1981
Year inducted into Hall of Fame: 1987

His real name is Charles Edward Greene, but to football fans he's known as "Mean" Joe Greene. He joined the Pittsburgh Steelers in 1969, and he was named the Defensive Rookie of the Year even though Pittsburgh had a record of only 1–13 that season. With Greene as the cornerstone of the franchise, Pittsburgh became the NFL's best team in the 1970s. He was named NFL Defensive Player of the Year in 1972 and 1974.

DICK LANE

81

Jersey number: 81
Position: Cornerback
Years in NFL: 1952–1965
Year inducted into Hall of Fame: 1974

Known by the nickname "Night Train," Dick Lane joined the Los Angeles Rams as a free agent in 1952 after four years in the U.S. Army. Football sources usually list him at 6'1" (1.85 m) and 194 pounds (88 kg), but he may have been bigger than that. He's considered the first "big man" to play the speed position of cornerback. Lane ranked second all-time in career interceptions with 68 when he retired in 1965 and still ranks fourth on the all-time list to this day.

REGGIE WHITE

92

Jersey number: 92
Position: Defensive end
Years in NFL: 1985–2000
Year inducted into Hall of Fame: 2006

Reggie White became an ordained minister at the age of 17, so naturally teammates began to call him the "Minister of Defense" at the University of Tennessee. White had more sacks (124) than games played (121) during his eight seasons with the Philadelphia Eagles. He later became the Green Bay Packers' all-time leader with 68.5 sacks. White was named the NFL's Defensive Player of the Year three times and was elected to 13 straight Pro Bowl games.

THE KICKING GAME

If the defense has stopped the offense from gaining a first down by the time it gets to fourth down (third down in Canada), the offensive team will usually kick the ball. If they are within 40 or so yards of the other team's end zone, they'll often line up for a field goal. If the kicker makes it, he scores three points for his team. If he misses, the other team takes possession at the kicking team's line of scrimmage.

If the offense is stopped too far away from the end zone to try a field goal, they'll have their punter try to kick the ball as far as he can toward the defensive team's end of the field. After the defensive team receives the punt, their team takes possession of the ball and goes on offense.

PUNTS AND PLACEKICKS

In football today, there are basically two ways to kick the ball: a punt or a place-kick. A punt is when a kicker drops the ball out of his hands and kicks it before it touches the ground. When a team punts, the ball is snapped from the center directly to the punter, who is standing deep in the backfield.

A placekick is made when a player kicks the ball from a fixed position on the ground. On a placekick for a field goal or an extra point after a touchdown, the ball is snapped by the center to a player in the backfield, the holder, who places the ball down on the ground and holds it upright for the kicker. When a placekick is for a kickoff, teams can use a kicking tee.

TO A TEE

Kicking a ball off a tee helps it go farther, which is why you'll often see an NFL kickoff go from the kicking team's own 35-yard line all the way through the far end zone.

From 1950 to 1988, kickers in U.S. college football were allowed to kick field goals off a small, flat kicking tee. High school football players are still allowed to use a two-inch (5-cm) kicking tee. Rules in the CFL allow for a one-inch (2.5-cm) tee. There have never been tees allowed for field goals in the NFL. The kicking tees allowed for kickoffs are designed very differently from the tees used for kicking field goals.

SCIENCE STUFF

By raising the ball slightly above the grass or turf with a kicking tee, the amount of friction is reduced in the first instant after the kicker's foot strikes the ball. Friction is a force applied to a ball in the opposite direction of its motion or intended motion. Even something as small and light as a few blades of grass pressing ever-so-slightly against the bottom of a football applies some force against the ball. So, raising a football slightly above the grass lessens the friction between the ball and the grass, and allows the ball to travel farther. Friction and gravity are what eventually stop a ball after it's been kicked or thrown. After a ball is kicked, it will continue moving, but its speed will gradually drop as a result of the friction against air. If someone was to kick a ball into outer space, where there is no friction, the ball would continue moving at a constant speed until it hit another object or some other force was applied against it. So, in outer space, it could fly forever.

PUNTS AND PUNTERS

Punters put the foot in football! After one team has kicked the ball away on a punt play, a player on the other team has a chance to use their feet in a different way ... by running with the ball on a punt return. Usually, the returning team will place one or two players about 35 to 45 yards from the line of scrimmage. That player is often a wide receiver or a punt return specialist. His job is to catch the punt (or pick it up off the ground) and run with it as far as he can back toward the line of scrimmage before he's tackled. His team will take over on offense from the spot where he was stopped.

In American football, nobody actually has to return a punt. The receiving team can simply let the ball hit the ground and roll until it stops or until the other team touches the ball to end the play. Then the receiving team starts on offense from that spot. The punt returner can also signal (by raising one arm) for a fair catch. In that case, the players on the team who punted the ball must give the punt returner room to catch the ball. The punt returner doesn't get a chance to run back if he's called for a fair catch. Once the punt is caught, the play is over and his team goes on offense from the spot where he caught the ball. Also, if a punted ball rolls into the end zone, the receiving team gets to take the ball on their own 20-yard line. That's why you'll often see a punter angling the ball toward the sidelines to try and put it out of bounds inside the 20-yard line and trap the offense as deep as possible in its own end of the field.

CANADA RULES!

In Canadian football, if a punt goes into the end zone, the kicking team will score one point unless the receiving team can move the ball back out of the end zone. Canadian punters will sometimes try to kick the ball out of bounds before it reaches the end zone because it's often more important to push the other team as deep as possible into its own end rather than score any points.

On punt returns, Canadian players cannot call for a fair catch or let the ball roll to a stop. There always has to be a punt return. However, the players on the team that kicked the ball cannot come within five yards of the player trying to return the punt until the ball has been caught. If the punt returner is not given those five yards, an official will throw a flag on the play and call a "no yards" penalty.

PENCIL POWER

For a punter, the distance he can kick the ball is important, but his key statistic is punting average. To find a punting average you need to divide the total yardage from all of a kicker's punts by the number of punts he's made.

Here's the formula: Total yardage ÷ Number of punts = Punting average

For example, in 1940 Sammy Baugh set the NFL record for the highest punting average in one season at 51.40 yards. Baugh punted the ball 35 times for a total of 1,799 yards: 1,799 ÷ 35 = 51.4.

Shane Lechler holds the NFL record for career punting average. Over his 17-year career, he punted the ball 1,444 times for a total of 68,678 yards. Can you find Shane's career punting average?

And what if you have a punter's average and the number of kicks he's made, but you want to figure out his total yardage? No sweat. All you have to do is multiply the two numbers together.

Here's the formula: Punter's average × Number of kicks = Total yardage

For example, Andy Lee of the Carolina Panthers had an average of 63.00 yards on four kicks in a game on September 8, 2016.

63.00 × 4 = 252 yards

On October 11, 1998, Leo Araguz of the Oakland Raiders set a record with 16 punts in one game and averaged 44.31 yards per punt. His total yardage was also a one-game record. Can you figure it out?

ANSWERS FROM TOP TO BOTTOM:
Shane Lechler: 68,678 ÷ 1,444 = 47.56 average
Leo Araguz: 44.31 × 16 = 709 yards

HANG TIME

When punting a football, hang time matters. Hang time is the amount of time it takes from the instant the ball leaves the punter's foot until it either hits the ground or is caught by an opposing player. In other words, it's the amount of time that the ball is in the air.

Punts with little hang time are easier for the opposing team to return, since the kicking team doesn't get much time to surround the returner. The longer the hang time, the farther downfield the tacklers from the kicking team can get. Therefore, the return should be much shorter.

LONG KICKS

For punts and field goals, distance matters. And some kickers definitely have a leg up on the competition. Here's a look at the stats and stories behind some football players who really conquer when it comes to kicks.

CHRIS MILO

LONGEST PUNTS

CFL:	108 yards	Zenon Andrusyshyn (Toronto Argonauts, 1977) Chris Milo (Saskatchewan Roughriders, 2011)
U.S. college:	99 yards	Pat Brady (University of Nevada, 1950)
NFL:	98 yards	Steve O'Neal (New York Jets, 1969)

LONGEST FIELD GOALS

U.S. college:	69 yards	Ove Johansson (Abilene Christian University, 1976)
U.S. high school:	68 yards	Dirk Borgognone (Reno High School, 1985)
NFL:	66 yards	Justin Tucker (Baltimore Ravens, 2021)
CFL:	62 yards	Paul McCallum (Saskatchewan Roughriders, 2001)

JUSTIN TUCKER

STATSTARS

The first player in NFL history to make a field goal longer than 60 yards was Tom Dempsey of the New Orleans Saints with a 63-yarder on November 8, 1970. Dempsey played 11 seasons in the NFL from 1969 to 1979, but he was an unlikely kicking hero. He was born without any fingers on his right hand, and with no toes on his right foot, which was his kicking foot. Dempsey wore a special short shoe with an enlarged and flattened front. People always wondered if this unique shoe gave Dempsey a special advantage. He certainly didn't think so. "How about you try kicking a sixty-three-yard field goal to win [the game] with two seconds left," he once told reporters, "and you're wearing a square shoe. Oh, yeah, and no toes, either."

Still, in 1977, the NFL passed a new rule: Any shoe that is worn by a player with [a disability to] his kicking leg must have a kicking surface that conforms to that of a standard kicking shoe.

STAT STORY

The record for the longest punt in any type of football game was set by a Canadian university player, who kicked a ball 114 yards on September 24, 1966. Strangely, it took 53 years for the record to become official. Thomas Pinckard of the University of New Brunswick (UNB) lined up on his own 21-yard line. When his punt landed, it bounced over the heads of the returners and rolled all the way to the goal line, and then through the end zone. (Back in 1966, end zones in Canadian football were 25 yards long, not the 20 yards they are today.)

At the time, Pinckard's punt was recorded at 89 yards, which was the distance from his 21-yard line to the other team's goal line on a 110-yard field. For some reason, the distance through the end zone wasn't counted. Officials at UNB believed it should have been. In 2019, they completed a comprehensive review where they studied old blueprints of the stadium and collected sworn statements from teammates and game officials. Finally, the governing body for university sports in Canada agreed to add the extra 25 yards, giving Pinckard an all-time record of 114.

FIRST KICK

As a soccer goalie in Wylie, Texas, Sarah Fuller impressed her high school's football coach by kicking a soccer ball more than 60 yards. At Vanderbilt University in 2020, she won a conference championship in women's soccer and got a chance to play for the men's football team, too. Fuller became the first female to play in an NCAA Division I college football game on November 28, 2020, and completed a kickoff for Vanderbilt during the second half. Two weeks later, on December 12, 2020, Fuller kicked an extra point against the University of Tennessee to become the first female to score in a Division I game.

DIGIT-YOU-KNOW?

A missed field goal counts for one point in Canadian football—unless the defensive team can pick it up and run (or kick) the ball out of the end zone. It's the same rule for punts that go into the end zone. Missed field goals are never worth any points in American football.

TRY *THIS!*

Time to Kick It

Unless you're some kind of superhero in disguise, you're probably not ready to break any NFL records. Even so, let's see how long a field goal you can actually kick. You can also try competing against friends to see who can kick a ball the farthest.

1 Make sure the laces on the ball are turned away from your foot. If the laces are the last thing a kicker's foot touches, they can make the ball move unpredictably. That's why you'll always see the punter or the holder on a placekick turn the football so that the laces are facing in the opposite direction from where the kicker's foot will hit the ball. Keep the ball standing as straight up as possible.

2 When approaching the ball, place your non-kicking foot as close to the ball as you can. Pointing the toes of your "plant" foot directly at the goal posts helps to open up your hips and draw as much power as you can from the muscles in your torso and legs.

3 Aim your foot to hit the ball at a spot about four inches (10.2 cm) off the ground.

4 Kick the ball with the top of your foot, not your toes. This helps to provide power. The harder you kick the ball, the farther it should go.

Extending your arm on the side of your body opposite your kicking leg at about a 90-degree angle helps to keep your body in balance when you make your kick.

5 After you've kicked the ball a few times, see what happens when you use a different approach. Try placing the ball at a new angle or kicking it with a different part of your foot. Or maybe you need to run a few more steps toward the ball. Notice how the kick changes depending on your varied moves.

CHAPTER SIX

IT'S

SUPER!

Super Bowl Sunday, when the NFL's championship game is played, is practically a national holiday in the United States. Fans often watch the game at Super Bowl parties, and it's not uncommon for more than 100 million people to tune in and watch. Big audiences also watch important televised college games. In Canada, the population is only about one-tenth the size of the United States, but the CFL's championship game is a big draw, too.

HISTORY BY THE NUMBERS

Because the big game is played in the winter—it used to be played in January, but since 2004 it's in February—the Super Bowl has traditionally been held in southern cities where it's warmer. Not all the time, though. Detroit, Minneapolis (twice), and Indianapolis have all hosted the game in domed stadiums, and an outdoor game was held in New Jersey in 2014. Still, with sites already selected until 2024, these places will have hosted the most Super Bowl games by then.

Miami/South Florida	**11**
New Orleans	**11**
Los Angeles/Pasadena	**7**
Tampa	**5**
Arizona	**4**

THE SUPER BOWL *GETS STARTED*

For more than 40 years after it was formed in 1920, the NFL couldn't be sure it would be football's primary league. There were several other leagues rivaling the NFL. The most serious competitor came in 1960 with the birth of the American Football League. The AFL vied with the NFL for players and fans. It attracted players by offering bigger contracts, and it attracted fans with what people thought was a more exciting kind of football. The AFL played games in a wide-open style, with lots of passing. NFL teams of that time still liked to run the ball and control the game with tight defense.

In 1966, the NFL and the AFL agreed to merge to form one big league. Until 1970, they each played their own individual schedules with their own separate playoffs, but starting at the end of the 1966 season, the NFL champions began to meet the AFL champions for a special championship game.

WHY SO SUPER?

The first Super Bowl was played between the NFL's Green Bay Packers and the AFL's Kansas City Chiefs on January 15, 1967, after the 1966 regular season. It was officially known as the NFL-AFL Championship Game. But Lamar Hunt, who owned the Chiefs, had come up with a superb new name. His kids had been playing with a toy known as a Super Ball, and so he called the big game the Super Bowl.

WHY ROMAN NUMERALS?

Unlike the World Series, the Stanley Cup, the World Cup, or the NBA Finals, the Super Bowl is always designated by its number. However, instead of using regular numbers, the NFL uses Roman numerals, which are actually letters that can be combined to represent numbers.

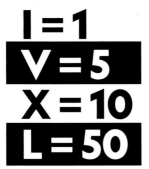

I = 1
V = 5
X = 10
L = 50

To create other numbers, you combine Roman numerals. So, for example, to represent 3, you put 1 together 3 times, so it is: III. XVI would be 16. LII is 52.

Other combinations can be trickier because when a letter of a smaller value is used in front of a letter of a higher value, it means you have to subtract. For example, an I in front of a V means 1 subtracted from 5. IV therefore means 4. Here are some other examples:

IX is 9.
XL means 10 subtracted from 50, so XL is 40.

To make higher numbers, you need to combine more and more letters. For example:

XXIX is 29
XLVIII is 48.

The idea of using numbers to mark the big game began with the fifth Super Bowl, or Super Bowl V, in 1971. Because the Super Bowl is played after New Year's Day, it takes place in the calendar year following the regular season. So, the Super Bowl played in 1971 decided the best team of the 1970 season. And instead of calling it the 1971 Super Bowl, they assigned it a Roman numeral to avoid confusion.

STATSTARS

Bryan Bartlett Starr—aka Bart Starr—sure lived up to his name. With Starr as their quarterback, the Packers were the best team in football throughout the 1960s. Starr led Green Bay to a 35–10 victory over Kansas City in the first Super Bowl game in 1967 and a 33–14 win over the Oakland Raiders in the second Super Bowl in 1968. The early Super Bowl passing records set by Starr have all been broken over the years, but he still holds the NFL's career record for passer rating throughout the playoffs. Starr put up a passer rating of 104.8 during his 10 career playoff games.

DIGIT-YOU-KNOW?

The only time the NFL used regular numbers for the Super Bowl was in 2016 for Super Bowl 50. Traditionally for weddings, 50 years marks a couple's golden anniversary. The NFL wanted to emphasize the Super Bowl's golden anniversary, so the logo for that year's Super Bowl featured the number 50 colored in gold.

SUPER FACTS AND FIGURES

It's not just the game that's super on Super Bowl Sunday. Even people who don't really like football sometimes watch it on TV. Why? Because each year advertisers use this TV time to showcase their best advertisements. These new commercials are known for being the funniest or the most likely to make you cry. They often feature big-name stars from movies and television. Also, a celebrity musician performs the national anthem before the game, and at halftime, there's a big concert featuring another popular musician. Still, for football fans, the game is king. Who's going to win? Which players will rise to the occasion? Who will crack under the pressure? That's what makes Super Bowl Sunday so exciting.

103,985

The highest attendance at a Super Bowl game was at Super Bowl XIV on January 20, 1980. The game was held at the Rose Bowl in Pasadena, California, with the nearby Los Angeles Rams facing off against the Pittsburgh Steelers. The Steelers won the game 31–19. Until COVID-19 restrictions limited the crowd to 22,000 people at Super Bowl LV in Tampa in 2021, the lowest attendance was 61,946 at Super Bowl I in Memorial Coliseum in Los Angeles.

114,442,000

The highest average TV audience in Super Bowl history was for Super Bowl XLIX on February 1, 2015. The New England Patriots beat the Seattle Seahawks 28–24. With more than 114 million people watching, it's not just the highest-rated Super Bowl; it's the highest-rated show in television history!

49–26

The highest scoring Super Bowl game was Super Bowl XXIX played on January 29, 1995. The San Francisco 49ers beat the San Diego Chargers 49–26 for a combined total of 75 points. San Francisco also holds the record for the most points by one team when they beat the Denver Broncos 55–10 in Super Bowl XXIV on January 28, 1990.

$15,000

The players on the championship team earned a $15,000 bonus from Super Bowl I to Super Bowl XI. By Super Bowl 50, the players on the Denver Broncos—that year's champions—earned a bonus of $102,000.

$5,000,000

The cost to run a 30-second commercial during the Super Bowl hit $5 million for the first time at Super Bowl LII in 2018. The cost to companies wanting to run a commercial during Super Bowl I in 1967 had been between $37,500 and $42,500.

EAT UP!

According to research done before Super Bowl 50 in 2016, more food is eaten in American homes on Super Bowl Sunday than on any other day of the year except Thanksgiving. That number includes approximately 1.3 billion chicken wings.

THE ROAD TO THE SUPER BOWL:
NFL PLAYOFFS

Before a team has a chance to win the Super Bowl, they have to make it through the playoffs. Since the 2020 season, 14 out of 32 teams make the playoffs: 7 in the AFC and 7 in the NFC. In each of those two conferences, all four division champions—the teams with the best regular-season win-loss record in each division—are guaranteed a playoff spot. The four division champions in each conference are ranked from 1 to 4 based on their regular-season records. Three wild card teams also make the playoffs in each conference. A wild card team is a team that gains a spot in a playoff or tournament despite not qualifying in the usual way.

In the NFL, the wild card teams are the three teams in each conference that have the best records but didn't win their divisions. The wild card teams are ranked 5, 6, and 7, even if one or more of them has a better record than another team that won a different division. If two or more teams are tied with the same record, there is a complicated tie-breaking system to determine who gets a playoff spot or a higher seeding in the playoffs. Throughout the playoffs, the higher seeded team is always the home team.

The NFL playoffs begin with the wild card round. This involves the teams in each conference ranked, or seeded, 2 through 7, with team 2 playing team 7, team 3 playing team 6, and team 4 playing team 5. The top seed in each conference gets a bye, or pass, directly into the second round of the playoffs, which is known as the divisional round. In the divisional round, the teams seeded number one that got the bye now face the lowest seeded teams to win in the wild card round, while the other two winners from the wild card round face each other in another game. The winners of the divisional round in each conference meet the following week to play for the conference championship. Two weeks later, the AFC champion faces the NFC champion in the Super Bowl.

EARLY CHAMPIONS

There were no playoffs in the NFL's early years. From 1920 until 1932, the championship team was the one that finished the regular season with the best record. The championship didn't necessarily go to the team with the most wins, but to the team that won the highest percentage of the games it played. It could be confusing. Four times in the league's first six seasons, there were disagreements about who was the championship team.

After all those arguments, the first NFL playoff game was played in 1932 to break a first-place tie between the Chicago Bears and the Portsmouth Spartans of Ohio. The Bears won it. Since 1933, the NFL has used playoff games to determine the league champion.

PATRICK MAHOMES MAKES A PASS UNDER PRESSURE DURING A 2020 PLAYOFF GAME.

NFL PLAYOFFS FORMAT

WILD CARD ROUND

DIVISIONAL ROUND

CONFERENCE CHAMPIONSHIP

AFC

#1 SEED (BYE WEEK)

#2 SEED
#7 SEED (WILD CARD)

#3 SEED
#6 SEED (WILD CARD)

#4 SEED
#5 SEED (WILD CARD)

#1 SEED

Lowest-seeded winner from AFC wild card round

Highest-seeded winner from AFC wild card round

Other winner from AFC wild card round

AFC CHAMPION

NFC

#1 SEED (BYE WEEK)

#2 SEED
#7 SEED (WILD CARD)

#3 SEED
#6 SEED (WILD CARD)

#4 SEED
#5 SEED (WILD CARD)

#1 SEED

Lowest-seeded winner from NFC wild card round

Highest-seeded winner from NFC wild card round

Other winner from NFC wild card round

NFC CHAMPION

SUPER BOWL CHAMPION

HISTORY BY THE NUMBERS

FIRST NFL CHAMPIONSHIP GAME:
Chicago Bears defeat New York Giants, 23–21 (1933)

MOST NFL CHAMPIONSHIPS:
11 – Green Bay Packers (1929, 1930, 1931, 1936, 1939, 1944, 1961, 1962, 1965, 1966, 1967)

MOST CONSECUTIVE CHAMPIONSHIPS:
3 – Green Bay Packers (1929, 1930, 1931 and 1965, 1966, 1967)

MOST POINTS BY ONE TEAM IN ONE GAME:
73 – Chicago Bears (Washington 0), 1940

MOST POINTS BY BOTH TEAMS IN ONE GAME:
73 – Detroit Lions 59, Cleveland Browns 14 (1957)

COLLEGE BOWL GAMES

Every year, around the end of December, there's a whole bunch of college football games on TV. They have names like the Liberty Bowl or the Citrus Bowl. You'll even see some brand names you might recognize, like the Cheez-It Bowl or the Outback Bowl.

But why are they even called bowl games when the game is football, not bowling? The name comes from the meaning of the word "bowl" (yes, like the thing you eat cereal out of at breakfast). In 1913, Yale University began construction of a new football stadium. When it opened in 1914, it was the first round stadium in the United States, and because of that bowl shape, it's always been known as the Yale Bowl. The word "bowl" soon caught on for other stadiums and for the big college football games, too—even if the stadiums they're played in aren't called bowls.

A ROSE BY ANY OTHER NAME

The Rose Bowl game is traditionally played on New Year's Day. It's been nicknamed "The Granddaddy of Them All" because it's college football's oldest bowl game. The first game was played on January 1, 1902. It has been played annually since 1916, but the game wasn't actually called the Rose Bowl until New Year's Day in 1923. That's the first time it was held at the brand-new Rose Bowl stadium. The stadium was called the Rose Bowl because Pasadena is known as the City of Roses and has hosted a Rose Parade on New Year's Day since 1890. The big football game took its new name from the stadium.

THE HALFTIME SHOW BEFORE A BIG CROWD AT THE ROSE BOWL GAME

FLORIDA STATE UNIVERSITY VERSUS AUBURN UNIVERSITY IN A CHAMPIONSHIP GAME AT THE ROSE BOWL

THE UNIVERSITY OF GEORGIA CELEBRATES AT THE 2020 SUGAR BOWL.

MORE TEAMS, MORE GAMES

For most of the 1900s, college bowl games were reserved for only the very best college teams in the United States. There was only the Rose Bowl until the 1930s, and there were still only about 12 bowl games each year well into the 1970s. Teams had to have a really good record during the season to qualify.

With more and more sports on television over the years, the NCAA thought it would be a good idea to have more bowl games to broadcast. So, starting in 2006, the NCAA changed the rules. Nowadays, teams don't have to have more wins than losses to qualify for a bowl game. By the 2010–2011 season, there were 35 bowl games featuring 70 different teams. In 2015–2016, there were 80 teams playing in 40 bowl games. Six of those 40 bowl games are still reserved for the very best teams. Those games are the Rose Bowl, the Sugar Bowl, the Orange Bowl, the Cotton Bowl, the Fiesta Bowl, and the Peach Bowl.

DIGIT-YOU-KNOW?

The University of Michigan defeated Stanford University 49–0 in the first Rose Bowl game in 1902. A few teams matched Michigan's 49-point total after that, but no team scored more than 49 points in the Rose Bowl for 113 years until the University of Oregon defeated Florida State University 59–20 in 2015.

NCAA CHAMPIONS

For many years, the top level of college football was the only NCAA-sponsored sport without an official championship playoff. There had been unofficial attempts to choose a college champion since 1901, but the first true effort to determine an official national champ began with the Associated Press in 1936 when they created the Associated Press (AP) Poll.

Since 1936, writers and broadcasters from all across the United States have contributed to the AP Poll. Originally, the Associated Press ranked the top 20 teams, but the poll expanded to the top 25 in 1989. Teams are ranked based on their records and on the strength of their opponents. The rankings can also be influenced simply by the opinions of the various voters. There are currently 62 writers and broadcasters who participate from all parts of the country. These journalists must be members of the Associated Press who cover college football regularly. Each of the 62 AP voters ranks his or her top 25 teams every week during the season. Those individual rankings are then combined to produce a national ranking. This is done by giving a team 25 points for each first-place vote it receives, 24 points for second ... all the way down to one point for a 25th-place vote. Then the team with the highest points total is ranked number one.

ISAIAH DAVIS
OF SOUTH DAKOTA
STATE UNIVERSITY

THE BCS

In 1992, an agreement was reached with four different college bowls to try to crown a true national champion. However, the Rose Bowl refused to participate, which meant not all of the country's best teams could vie for the championship. In 1998, the Bowl Championship Series (BCS) was created. The BCS used a combination of the AP Top 25 polls and a computer ranking system to create matchups involving 10 top teams. From 1998 to 2006, one of these four bowl games—the Rose Bowl, the Fiesta Bowl, the Sugar Bowl, or the Orange Bowl—would always feature the teams ranked #1 and #2 playing for the championship. From 2007 until 2013, the separate BCS National Championship Game was held after the four Bowl Games.

THE UNIVERSITY
OF ALABAMA
TAKES THE FIELD

COLLEGE FOOTBALL PLAYOFF

Finally, in 2014, a true championship play-off was created. A 13-member selection committee chooses four top teams to take part in the College Football Playoff. Any two of the Rose Bowl, Sugar Bowl, Orange Bowl, Cotton Bowl, Fiesta Bowl, or Peach Bowl are used each year for the semifinal games. The team ranked #1 will play #4 in one of those bowl games, while the teams ranked #2 and #3 will meet in another. Both semifinal games are played on the same day. The two winners meet in the College Football Playoff played on the first Monday that is six days or more after the semifinals.

LOUISIANA STATE UNIVERSITY CELEBRATES A NATIONAL CHAMPIONSHIP.

PENCIL POWER

Heading into the College Football Playoff in January 2020, Clemson University, Louisiana State University (LSU), Ohio State University, and the University of Oklahoma were the top four teams in the final AP Poll. Their voting stats are listed below.

To figure out their points, the formula is this:

(1st place votes × 25) + (2nd place votes × 24) + (3rd place votes × 23) + (4th place votes × 22)

If a team didn't get any votes in a particular category, you don't need to include that number.

So, using Clemson as an example, the formula would be:

(3 × 25) + (9 × 24) + (50 × 23) = 75 + 216 + 1,150 = 1,441.

Can you figure out how many points the three other teams had, and then list all four teams by their ranking?

TEAM	1ST PLACE VOTES	2ND PLACE VOTES	3RD PLACE VOTES	4TH PLACE VOTES
CLEMSON	3	9	50	0
LSU	47	15	0	0
OHIO STATE	12	38	12	0
OKLAHOMA	0	0	0	62

SPENCER RATTLER OF THE UNIVERSITY OF OKLAHOMA

ANSWERS:

LSU: (47 × 25) + (15 × 24) = 1,175 + 360 = 1,535
Ohio State: (12 × 25) + (38 × 24) + (12 × 23) = 300 + 912 + 276 = 1,488
Oklahoma: 62 × 22 = 1,364.
Rankings:
#1 LSU   #2 Ohio State   #3 Clemson   #4 Oklahoma

CANADA'S CHAMPIONSHIP

Football teams in Canada have been chasing after their championship trophy for a lot longer than American teams have been trying to win the Super Bowl. Although there are only nine teams in the CFL, the playoff champions from the East Division face the playoff champions from the West Division. They play for the same trophy today that Canadian champions have hoped to capture since 1909. That trophy—and the game itself—is known as the Grey Cup.

THE CFL SETUP

Like American football, Canadian football began in the 1860s, but it was reorganized in the 1880s. Officially, the CFL didn't begin until 1958, but most of the teams in the league are a lot older than that.

The CFL's East Division is made up of the Toronto Argonauts, the Hamilton Tiger-Cats, the Montreal Alouettes, and the Ottawa Redblacks. The Argonauts and teams representing these other three cities have been playing together since 1907. The CFL West Division features the British Columbia Lions, the Calgary Stampeders, the Edmonton Elks, the Winnipeg Blue Bombers, and the Saskatchewan Roughriders.

The top three teams in each division make the playoffs for the CFL, but if the fourth-place team in one of the divisions has a better record than the third-place team in the other, they get to crossover into the other division and join their top two teams in the playoffs. The team that finishes in second place in each division plays at home against the third-place team or the crossover team in the Eastern and Western Semifinals. The two first-place teams have a bye week, and then host the semifinal winners in the Eastern Final and the Western Final. The winners of those two games meet the next week for the Grey Cup.

THE ARGONAUTS VERSUS THE ROUGHRIDERS

PENCIL POWER

If the first Super Bowl was played in 1967 and the first Grey Cup game was played in 1909, how much older is the Grey Cup than the Super Bowl? What would your answer be in Roman numerals?

ANSWERS: 1967 − 1909 = 58, LVIII

GREY CUP FACTS AND FIGURES

MOST WINS:
17 - TORONTO ARGONAUTS

(1914, 1921, 1933, 1937, 1938, 1945, 1946, 1947, 1950, 1952, 1983, 1991, 1996, 1997, 2004, 2012, 2017)

MOST CONSECUTIVE WINS:
5 - EDMONTON ELKS

(1978, 1979, 1980, 1981, 1982)

MOST POINTS IN ONE GAME BY ONE TEAM:
54 - QUEEN'S UNIVERSITY (REGINA 0) (1923)

MOST POINTS BY BOTH TEAMS IN ONE GAME:
83 - SASKATCHEWAN ROUGHRIDERS 43, HAMILTON TIGER-CATS 40 (1989)

CALGARY VERSUS TORONTO

HISTORY BY THE NUMBERS

The first Grey Cup game was played on December 4, 1909. The University of Toronto defeated the Parkdale Canoe Club, 26–6. Canada's participation in World War I resulted in the cancellation of the Grey Cup from 1916 until 1918. Competition didn't resume until 1920. Teams from western Canada were allowed to participate for the first time in 1921. The Toronto Argonauts beat Edmonton 23–0 that year for the first Grey Cup shutout.

From 1942 to 1945, during World War II, military teams were allowed to compete for the Grey Cup. Since 1946, the game has always featured an East-West format. Since 1954, only teams that are in the CFL have competed for the Grey Cup.

FANTASY FOOTBALL

You've learned all about the basics of football IRL (in real life). You've learned about players and their statistics and the championships they chase. Now it's time to use what you've learned to compete for a championship of your own in fantasy football.

What's that? Fantasy football is a math-based game using real-life players' statistics. It typically involves players in the NFL; however, in some leagues, people select the CFL or college players.

Fans playing fantasy football get to draft their own teams. As the weeks go by, they can add players to their roster—as long as no one else in their league has picked them yet. Since rosters usually have a set size, you'll likely have to drop someone from your lineup to add someone new. You can also trade for players from other teams in your league. Some fantasy football leagues run for years. Others only go week to week. Many fantasy leagues start up each season with a brand-new draft of players.

Fantasy football teams usually include a roster of 15 players who play real positions like this:

1	Quarterback	(QB)
2	Running backs	(RB)
2	Wide receivers	(WR)
1	Tight end	(TE)
1	Placekicker	(PK)
1	Team defense	(D)
1	Flex player	(usually RB or WR)
6	Bench players	(substitutes)

Players on a fantasy football team generate points based on their performance in actual league games. Some fantasy football leagues only count points scored from touchdowns or field goals, but most leagues use a combination of points scored and statistics. So, if the QB on the Rams scores a touchdown and he's on your team, you get to put six points on your chart. If you've got a running back from the Ravens and he rushes for 100 yards even without a touchdown, you score points for that, too. A typical fantasy football league might score points like this:

1 point for every 25 yards a quarterback passes

1 point for every 10 rushing yards

1 point for every 10 receiving yards

1 point for every extra point kicked

1 point per sack by a defensive player

2 points for an interception or a fumble recovery

3 points for each field goal up to 39 yards long

4 points for each field goal from 40 to 49 yards

5 points for each field goal from 50+ yards

6 points for each touchdown scored

4 points for throwing a touchdown pass

Some fantasy leagues have a new winner every week, but lots of them add up the points over an entire season.

DEANDRE HOPKINS

PENCIL POWER

Suppose you had these three players on your 15-man fantasy football team, and they had these statistics in their last game:

QB – Russell Wilson	308 yards passing, 22 yards rushing, 3 touchdown passes
RB – Ezekiel Elliott	123 yards rushing, 14 yards receiving, 1 touchdown
WR – DeAndre Hopkins	132 yards receiving, 2 touchdowns

Using the point system on this page, can you figure out how many points they scored for you?

EZEKIEL ELLIOTT

ANSWERS: Wilson

308 yards passing ÷ 25 = 12.32 so   12 points
22 yards rushing ÷ 10 = 2.2 so   2 points
3 touchdown passes x 4 =   12 points
         26 points

Elliott   123 yards rushing ÷ 10 = 12.3 so   12 points
14 yards receiving ÷ 10 = 1.4 so   1 point
1 touchdown x 6 =   6 points
         19 points

Hopkins   132 yards receiving ÷ 10 = 13.2 so   13 points
2 touchdowns x 6 =   12 points
         25 points

26 + 19 + 25 = 70 points

TRY *THIS!*

Lights, Camera, Football!

Do you love talking about football with your friends? Wish you had your own sports talk show or football podcast to share your thoughts on players and how you think your favorite team is going to do in the upcoming season? Let's make those dreams happen! Get ready to brush up on your reading skills, clear your voice, and get camera-ready, because it's time to talk football.

1 Sit down with your friend and choose 15 players you want to learn more about. They can be professional or college players, still playing or retired. You can choose 15 people who all played the same position, or you can make a list that covers every position on a team. Choose athletes who play on the NFL or CFL team closest to where you live, or who play in a city you've always wanted to visit.

2 Once you have your list of 15, ask an adult to help you find news articles about the people on your list. You can even see if your local library has any books about them.

3 Grab your calendar and assign one player to each day for 15 days in a row. On each day, you and your friend can read the articles or books you found about that player for about 15 minutes. Use this book to help decode any statistics or football terms used.

4 After the 15 days are up, and you've learned everything you can about your set of 15 players, it's show time! Get together with your friend and come up with a fun name for your podcast or talk show. After you hit "record," introduce yourselves and the show, and then dive into your list of players and what you learned from all the reading and research you did. Once the show's a wrap, share it with your family and friends and see what they think! Did they learn something new? Do they agree with your super football analysis?

CHAPTER SEVEN

10 CRAZY NUMBERS

In football the numbers never end. We've looked at passing, running, and defensive statistics, but here are 10 more numbers you should know—one for each yard it takes to get a first down. So, if you want to become a football expert, strap on your helmet and let's get in the game.

DIGIT-YOU-KNOW?

The Pro Football Hall of Fame opened in Canton, Ohio, in 1963. There were 17 men voted in that year, which was the largest class of Hall of Famers elected at one time until 2020 when 20 new members were selected to honor the 100th anniversary of the NFL. Over the years, the Chicago Bears have had more Hall of Famers elected than any other team with a total of 36.

0-0

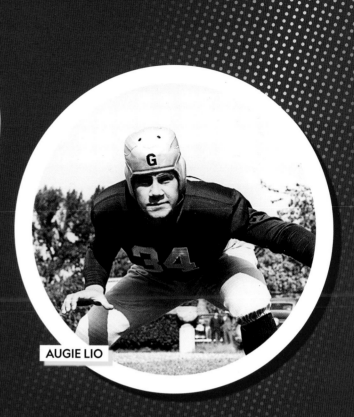

AUGIE LIO

Seventy-three games in early NFL history ended in a scoreless tie. The last 0–0 game was played on November 7, 1943, when the Detroit Lions hosted the New York Giants on a cold, wet day with a slick, sloppy field. There were only nine first downs, with the Lions recording 130 yards in net offense (102 rushing, 28 passing) while the Giants managed only 84 (81 rushing, 3 passing). Lions kicker Augie Lio missed three field goals in the game. Giants kicker Ward Cuff missed one.

STAT STORY

The NFL has had 59 games with a final score of 3-0. Seven of those have been played since the last scoreless tie in 1943. The most recent game was on November 26, 2007, when the Pittsburgh Steelers beat the Miami Dolphins 3-0. In two of the other six games, the winning field goal was kicked by the same player, Neil O'Donoghue.

O'Donoghue was 6'6" (1.98 m) tall, which makes him the tallest kicker in NFL history. O'Donoghue played in the NFL with the Buffalo Bills, the Tampa Bay Buccaneers, and the St. Louis Cardinals between 1977 and 1985. For Buffalo on October 16, 1977, he kicked a second-quarter field goal in a 3-0 win over the Atlanta Falcons. A little more than two years later, on December 16, 1979, O'Donoghue kicked a fourth-quarter field goal to lead Tampa Bay past Kansas City 3-0.

Fewest Points Scored, CFL Game

1 point–Montreal defeats Ottawa, 1–0 (Oct. 30, 1966)
2 points–Ottawa ties Toronto, 1–1 (Nov. 3, 1928)
- Toronto defeats Montreal, 2–0 (Oct. 11, 1930)
- Toronto defeats Hamilton, 2–0 (Sept. 20, 1947)

HINES WARD OF THE STEELERS IN THEIR 3-0 WIN OVER MIAMI

222

The highest scoring game in football history is pretty hard to believe. On October 7, 1916, Georgia Tech beat Cumberland College of Lebanon, Tennessee, U.S.A., 222–0! Georgia Tech had 32 touchdowns and kicked 30 extra points. Cumberland never made a first down. Georgia Tech scored 10 touchdowns on first downs and never needed more than three downs to score. Cumberland never gained 10 yards on any four downs. In fairness to the Cumberland players, their school didn't have a true football program at this time. Their team was really only a group put together to play a few games.

GEORGIA TECH PLAYING CUMBERLAND COLLEGE IN 1916

THE 1916 GEORGIA TECH FOOTBALL TEAM

CENTURY SCORES

College football games in which one team scored at least 100 points happened fairly often between the 1880s and the 1920s. They were sometimes referred to as "century scores" because a century is 100 years.

Since the 1880s, there have been about 200 games where a team scored 100 points, but these lopsided scores have been a lot rarer since the 1930s. In fact, there have only been three in the last 50 years. The most recent occurred in 2003 when Rockford University (in Rockford, Illinois, U.S.A.) beat Trinity Bible College (in Ellendale, North Dakota, U.S.A.) 105–0.

32

It's pretty exciting to watch your team rally for a victory. Imagine how excited Buffalo Bills fans were when their team rallied from a 32-point deficit to beat the Houston Oilers in an AFC playoff game on January 3, 1993. It's the biggest comeback in NFL history.

Frank Reich (who went on to become coach of the Indianapolis Colts in 2018) was making his first playoff start that day in place of injured quarterback Jim Kelly. Things didn't go well for a while, as Houston outscored Buffalo 28–3 by halftime. The Oilers scored again after a 58-yard interception return for a touchdown early in the third quarter to go ahead 35–3 for a 32-point lead. After that, it was all Bills. A short touchdown run followed by four Frank Reich touchdown (TD) passes put Buffalo on top 38–35 in the fourth quarter. A late Houston field goal tied the game, but the Bills won it 41–38 in overtime.

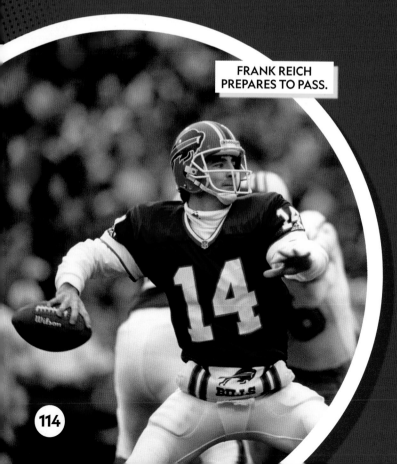

FRANK REICH PREPARES TO PASS.

PENCIL POWER

Given the scoring summary below, and what you know about how many points a touchdown, a field goal, and an extra point are worth, can you figure out the score quarter by quarter during Buffalo's record rally against Houston?

1ST QUARTER:

Houston — TD Haywood Jeffires 3-yard pass from Warren Moon
(Al Del Greco kick)
Buffalo — FG Steve Christie 36 yards

2ND QUARTER:

Houston — TD Webster Slaughter 7-yard pass from Moon
(Del Greco kick)
Houston — TD Curtis Duncan 26-yard pass from Moon
(Del Greco kick)
Houston — TD Jeffires 27-yard pass from Moon
(Del Greco kick)

3RD QUARTER:

Houston — TD Bubba McDowell 58-yard interception return
(Del Greco kick)
Buffalo — TD Kenneth Davis 1-yard run
(Christie kick)
Buffalo — TD Don Beebe 38-yard pass from Reich
(Christie kick)
Buffalo — TD Andre Reed 26-yard pass from Reich
(Christie kick)
Buffalo — TD Reed 18-yard pass from Reich
(Christie kick)

4TH QUARTER:

Buffalo — TD Reed 17-yard pass from Reich
(Christie kick)
Houston — FG Del Greco 26 yards

OVERTIME:

Buffalo — FG Christie 32 yards

113

On November 27, 1966, Washington and the New York Giants set an NFL record when they combined for 16 touchdowns and set an all-time scoring record with 113 points in a 72–41 Washington victory. Washington tied the NFL record with 10 touchdowns that day and set a new regular-season record with 72 points. That left them one point short of the all-time scoring record of 73 points set by the Chicago Bears when they beat Washington 73–0 in the 1940 NFL championship game.

WASHINGTON'S A. D. WHITFIELD SCORES A TOUCHDOWN.

MOST POINTS SCORED BY BOTH TEAMS, NFL:

113 – Washington 72, New York Giants 41 (Nov. 27, 1966)

106 – Cincinnati Bengals 58, Cleveland Browns 48 (Nov. 28, 2004)

105 – Los Angeles Rams 54, Kansas City Chiefs 51 (Nov. 19, 2018)

101 – New Orleans Saints 52, New York Giants 49 (Nov. 1, 2015)

101 – Oakland Raiders 52, Houston Oilers 49 (Dec. 22, 1963)

MOST POINTS SCORED BY BOTH TEAMS, CFL:

111 – Toronto 68, British Columbia 43 (Sept. 1, 1990)

MOST POINTS SCORED BY ONE TEAM, CFL:

82 – Montreal vs. Hamilton (14) (Oct. 20, 1956)

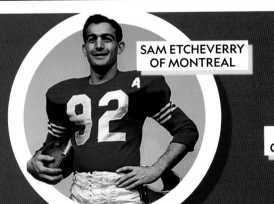

SAM ETCHEVERRY OF MONTREAL

MIKE "PINBALL" CLEMONS OF TORONTO

13

Green Bay is the smallest city with a team in the NFL. The population is barely more than 105,000, and yet Lambeau Field, the Packers' home stadium, can hold 81,441 fans. Green Bay is also one of the northernmost cities in the NFL. The weather can get pretty cold there, especially come playoff time. People sometimes refer to Lambeau's natural turf field as the "Frozen Tundra." That nickname began after Green Bay hosted the Dallas Cowboys in the NFL championship game on December 31, 1967. The game itself has been dubbed the "Ice Bowl."

According to the NFL record book, the temperature in Green Bay was 13° below zero Fahrenheit (–25°C). The field truly was frozen, and the weather was so cold the referees couldn't use their metal whistles because they froze to their lips! (They had to shout out their calls instead.) Packers linebacker Ray Nitschke developed frostbite in his feet, which caused his toes to turn purple. Quarterback Bart Starr had frostbite on his fingers by the end of the game. He still managed to hold onto the ball and plunge two feet for a last-second touchdown that gave Green Bay a 21–17 victory.

GREEN BAY PACKERS PLAYERS TRY TO STAY WARM DURING THE "ICE BOWL" GAME

CALGARY AND TORONTO PLAY IN THE SNOW.

CANADIAN ICE BOWL

Many CFL cities can be colder in winter than Green Bay, but despite the chill, the Grey Cup game is still held in November. (CFL seasons start in June, not September like the NFL, so they end earlier, too.) The coldest Grey Cup game on record was the 1991 Grey Cup in Winnipeg, Manitoba. The temperature at kickoff was –17°C. The Toronto Argos beat the Calgary Stampeders 36–21.

Still, the Grey Cup game that Canadians call the "Ice Bowl" was played at Montreal's Olympic Stadium in 1977 between the Edmonton Elks and the hometown Alouettes. Stadium workers used salt to melt the snow that had fallen on the artificial turf during a blizzard two days before the game. When the temperature plunged the next day, the melted snow turned into ice. Regular football shoes couldn't provide proper traction on the frozen field. Many Alouettes players attached staples to the bottoms of their shoes. It seemed to work. Montreal completely dominated Edmonton and won 41–6.

HOW COLD IS IT?

If you're curious about what that –13° Fahrenheit is in degrees Celsius, the formula to convert Fahrenheit into Celsius goes like this: You must subtract 32 from the number of degrees, and then multiply by 5 and divide by 9. Here's the formula:

Celsius temperature = (Fahrenheit temperature – 32) × 5/9

So, –13 – 32 = –45 and –45 × 5 = –225
–225 ÷ 9 = –25
So, –13°F = –25°C

HEAVY SNOW IN PHILADELPHIA
WHEN THE EAGLES FACED THE
DETROIT LIONS

PENCIL POWER

A simple way to approximate the temperature conversion from Celsius to Fahrenheit is to double the number and add 30. The actual formula is a little more complicated.

To convert a temperature in Celsius to a temperature in Fahrenheit, you need to multiply the number of degrees by 9, then divide that number by 5 and add 32.

Here's the formula: F = (9/5) C + 32

So if the temperature for the coldest Grey Cup was -17°C, can you calculate the temperature in degrees Fahrenheit?

Now how about some hot weather? A game between the New England Patriots and Jacksonville Jaguars in 2018 was played when it was 97°F. What's that in Celsius?

THE STEELERS IN THE
SNOW AND COLD OF
PITTSBURGH

BLAKE BORTLES

Answers:

Converting -17° Celsius to Fahrenheit
(-17° × 9/5) + 32.
-17° × 9 = -153. -153 ÷ 5 = -30.6. -30.6 + 32 = 1.4. So, -17°C equals 1.4°F.

Converting 97° Fahrenheit into Celsius
(97 – 32) × 5/9.
97 – 32 = 65. 65 × 5 = 325. 325 ÷ 9 = 36.11. So, 97°F equals 36.11°C.

26

George Blanda played a combined 26 seasons in the NFL and the American Football League from 1949 to 1975. That gives Blanda the longest career in pro football history. He was nearly 49 years old when he retired, making him the oldest player ever in the NFL. Blanda played for the Chicago Bears, the Baltimore Colts, the Houston Oilers, and the Oakland Raiders. He was a placekicker as well as a star quarterback. Blanda scored 2,002 points during his career, which was the most in history when he retired in 1975. His total stood as an NFL record for 25 years until it was broken by kicker Gary Anderson in 2000. Blanda still holds NFL records for kicking the most extra points after touchdowns (943) and for leading the league in extra points the most times (8).

STATSTARS

Jason Hanson set an NFL record for the longest career spent entirely with one team. Hanson joined the Detroit Lions in 1992 and had played with them for 21 seasons by the time he retired in 2012. During his career, Hanson kicked 52 field goals that were 50 yards or longer. That was an NFL record at the time but was broken by Sebastian Janikowski in 2016.

2,600

Adam Vinatieri might be the greatest place-kicker in NFL history. Vinatieri began his career in 1996 with the New England Patriots and played with the Indianapolis Colts from 2006 to 2019. On the last day of the 2018 NFL season, Vinatieri kicked a 25-yard field goal late in the game as part of the Colts' 33–17 win over the Tennessee Titans. Those three points gave Vinatieri a total of 2,600 in his career, which is a milestone no other player has ever achieved. The previous NFL scoring record of 2,544 points was held by kicker Morten Andersen, who played from 1982 to 2007. Vinatieri also broke Andersen's career record of 565 field goals in 2018. He made 599 field goals in his career and scored 2,695 points.

ADAM VINATIERI

8 MOST FIELD GOALS IN ONE GAME, NFL:
Rob Bironas, Tennessee Titans vs. Houston Texans (Oct. 21, 2007)

8 MOST FIELD GOALS IN ONE GAME, CFL:
Dave Ridgway, Saskatchewan vs. Ottawa (July 29, 1984)

Dave Ridgway, Saskatchewan vs. Edmonton (July 23, 1988)

Mark McLoughlin, Calgary vs. Saskatchewan (Aug. 5, 1996)

Paul Osbaldiston, Hamilton vs. Ottawa (Sept. 22, 1996)

ROB BIRONAS

7 MOST FIELD GOALS IN ONE GAME, NCAA:
Mike Prindle, Western Michigan vs. Marshall (Sept. 29, 1984)

Dale Klein, Nebraska vs. Missouri (Oct. 19, 1985)

31

LaDainian Tomlinson set an NFL record for most touchdowns in a season when he scored 31 touchdowns for the San Diego Chargers in 2006. The old record of 28 touchdowns had been set just one year before, by Shaun Alexander of the Seattle Seahawks. Tomlinson's touchdown total also helped him break another old record. His 186 points in 2006 broke Paul Hornung's scoring record of 176, which had lasted since 1960. Tomlinson rushed for more than 1,000 yards in each of his first eight seasons in the NFL from 2001 to 2008. In addition to his record total of 31 touchdowns in 2006, Tomlinson led the league with 1,815 rushing yards. His 28 rushing touchdowns (three more touchdowns came on passing plays) also set a new record. Not surprisingly, Tomlinson was named the NFL's MVP that season.

LADAINIAN TOMLINSON PLAYED 11 SEASONS IN THE NFL, MOSTLY WITH THE SAN DIEGO CHARGERS.

208

Jerry Rice holds the NFL career record for touchdowns with 208. No one else is even close. Second on the list is Emmitt Smith, who had 175 touchdowns in his career. Rice starred in the NFL for 20 seasons, mostly with the San Francisco 49ers, from 1985 to 2004. He caught 197 touchdown passes, rushed for 10 touchdowns, and scored one more on a fumble recovery. He also scored four two-point conversions in his career, giving him a total of 1,256 points. That's the most points of all time for any NFL player who is not a kicker. In addition to his touchdown record, Rice holds almost every career record for receiving.

JERRY RICE CELEBRATES A TOUCHDOWN.

147

MOST TOUCHDOWNS IN A CAREER, CFL	RUSH	REC	KICK RETURN
Milt Stegall, Winnipeg (1995–2008)	2	144	1

23

MOST TOUCHDOWNS IN A SEASON, CFL	RUSH	REC	KICK RETURN
Milt Stegall, Winnipeg (2002)	0	23	0

6

MOST TOUCHDOWNS IN A GAME, CFL	RUSH	REC	KICK RETURN
Bob McNamara, Winnipeg (vs. B.C., Oct. 13, 1956)	4	2	0

88

MOST TOUCHDOWNS IN A CAREER, NCAA*	RUSH	REC	KICK RETURN
Keenan Reynolds, Navy (2012–2015)	88	0	0

39

MOST TOUCHDOWNS IN A SEASON, NCAA*	RUSH	REC	KICK RETURN
Montee Ball, Wisconsin (2011)	33	6	0
Barry Sanders, Oklahoma State (1988)	37	0	2

8

MOST TOUCHDOWNS IN A GAME, NCAA*	RUSH	REC	KICK RETURN
Howard Griffith, Illinois (vs. Southern Illinois, Sept. 22, 1990)	8	0	0
Kalen Ballage, Arizona State (vs. Texas Tech, Sept. 10, 2016)	7	1	0

*records since 1956

1929

They say that records are made to be broken—but maybe that's not true. The oldest entry in the NFL record book is one that was set more than 90 years ago. In all that time, only two people have ever come close to breaking it.

On Thanksgiving Day, November 28, 1929, fullback Ernie Nevers gave fans of the Chicago Cardinals something to be thankful for. Nevers rushed for six touchdowns that day. He also kicked the extra point after four of those touchdowns, which gave him 40 points in total. Nevers accounted for all his team's scoring in a 40–6 victory over city rivals the Chicago Bears.

Not only is Nevers's 40 points in one game still an NFL record, he's also the only player in NFL history to score six rushing touchdowns in one game. Dub Jones (Cleveland Browns versus Chicago Bears, November 25, 1951) and Gale Sayers (Chicago Bears versus San Francisco 49ers, December 12, 1965) are the only other players in NFL history to score six touchdowns in a single game, but each of them only scored four rushing touchdowns.

Amazingly, just four days before his 40-point game, Ernie Nevers had scored all 19 points (three rushing touchdowns, one extra point) in the Cardinals' 19–0 victory over the Dayton Triangles, giving him 59 consecutive points for his team.

ERNIE NEVERS POSES FOR A PUBLICITY PHOTO IN 1930.

STAT STORY

In addition to football, Ernie Nevers played baseball and basketball while he was a student at Stanford University. While playing pro football in the NFL, Nevers also pitched in Major League Baseball. He played in some games for three seasons with the old St. Louis Browns from 1926 to 1928. In 1927, he gave up two home runs to Babe Ruth when Ruth set what was then a Major League record of 60 home runs. Nevers didn't have an extraordinary baseball career, but he was an All-League all-star in all five of his NFL seasons. In 1963, he became a charter member of the Pro Football Hall of Fame despite playing only 54 NFL games. That's the fewest games by any player ever enshrined in the football hall.

ERNIE NEVERS AS A ROOKIE PITCHER IN 1926

NICK FOLES

HISTORY BY THE NUMBERS

No one has ever scored seven touchdowns in one NFL game, but these eight quarterbacks have all thrown seven touchdown passes:

Sid Luckman, Chicago Bears	vs.	New York Giants (Nov. 14, 1943)
Adrian Burk, Philadelphia Eagles	vs.	Washington (Oct. 17, 1954)
George Blanda, Houston Oilers	vs.	New York Titans (Nov. 19, 1961)
Y. A. Tittle, New York Giants	vs.	Washington (Oct. 28, 1962)
Joe Kapp, Minnesota Vikings	vs.	Baltimore Colts (Sept. 28, 1969)
Peyton Manning, Denver Broncos	vs.	Baltimore Ravens (Sept. 5, 2013)
Nick Foles, Philadelphia Eagles	vs.	Oakland Raiders (Nov. 4, 2013)
Drew Brees, New Orleans Saints	vs.	New York Giants (Nov. 1, 2015)

PEYTON MANNING

DREW BREES

FOOTBALL GLOSSARY

acceleration: building up speed in a short amount of time

backfield: the offensive team's area behind the line of scrimmage; also the group of offensive players who line up there

block/blocking: one or more players using their body to get in the way of another player

blitz: when a higher number of defensive players than usual (often four or more) rush the quarterback on a passing play

circumference: the distance around the edge of a circle or other round object

crossbar: the post that is parallel to the ground on a goal post. The ball must go over it to count for points.

down: the period of a play in football

end zone: the area beyond the goal line at either end of the field where teams score touchdowns; in American football, the end zones are 10 yards long, and in Canadian football, they are 20 yards.

fair catch: when a punt returner lifts his arm to signal that he will not try to run with the ball once he's caught it

goal posts: the posts that the ball must be kicked through on a field goal or a try for an extra point after a touchdown. Goal posts are in the back of the end zone in American football and on the goal line in Canadian football.

gridiron: another name for a football field; it is named so because the lines on the field make it look similar to a metal grid or grill used for cooking.

kickoff: a kick that puts the ball in play at the start of each half, at the start of overtime, following an extra point attempt after a touchdown, and after a successful field goal

long bomb: a pass thrown deep down the field to try to gain a lot of yards, also known as a Hail Mary

PAT/extra point/conversion/convert: the different names for the play when a team tries to score an extra point after a touchdown. Teams can try to kick the ball through the goal posts to score one extra point or can try to run or pass the ball into the end zone to score two extra points.

penalty: when a player does something that is against the rules; game officials throw a flag when they see a penalty occur.

pick/pick 6: when a player on the defensive team catches a pass intended for an offensive player, also called an interception. If an interception is run back for a touchdown, it is sometimes called a "pick 6" for the six points scored.

playoffs: games played after the regular season that lead to the league championships

red zone: the area at either end of the field between the goal line and the 20-yard line

roster: the list of players on a team

sack: when a quarterback is tackled behind the line of scrimmage on a passing play

scramble/scrambler: when a quarterback runs around behind the line of scrimmage, trying to avoid being sacked. A scrambler is someone who is very good at doing this.

scrimmage line/line of scrimmage: the line where every offensive play in a football game begins, with the ball placed on the field and the two teams lined up facing each other. The scrimmage line is actually just an imaginary line—although TV graphics sometimes display it when you watch a game.

seed/seeding: the position of a team's ranking for the playoffs

snap: each down begins with a player known as the center snapping the ball (passing it backward between his legs) directly to another player on his team (usually the quarterback) lined up behind the line of scrimmage

tackle: the way football players grab hold of a ballcarrier and try to knock them down

uprights: the tallest parts of the goal post, which extend up from the crossbar. The ball must go in between the two uprights to count for points.

velocity: the speed something moves

wild card: a team that gains a spot in a playoff or tournament despite not qualifying in the usual way. In the NFL, the wild card teams are the two teams in each conference that have the best record among all the teams that didn't finish in first place in their divisions.

LEAGUE ABBREVIATIONS

AFC: American Football Conference

AFL: American Football League

CFL: Canadian Football League

NCAA: National Collegiate Athletic Association

NFC: National Football Conference

NFL: National Football League

POSITION ABBREVIATIONS

CB: Cornerback

DB: Defensive back

DE: Defensive end

DT: Defensive tackle

FB: Fullback

HB: Halfback

K: Kicker

LB: Linebacker

LG/RG: Left guard/Right guard

LT/RT: Left tackle/Right tackle

OT: Offensive tackle

P: Punter

PK: Placekicker

QB: Quarterback

RB: Running back

S: Safety

TE: Tight end

WR: Wide receiver

CREDITS

AS = Adobe Stock; GI = Getty Images; SS = Shutterstock

Cover: (UP CTR), Joseph W. Pyle/SS; (helmet), Gino Santa Maria/SS; (field), TAlex/AS; (UP RT), Daniel Padavona/SS; (LO RT), mtsaride/AS; (LO LE), OSTILL is Franck Camhi/SS; (CTR LE), Pete Saloutos/GI; **Spine:** (LO RT), mtsaride/AS; **Back cover:** (UP RT), archideaphoto/SS; (chalkboard), mexrix/SS; (LO RT), Brocreative/SS; (LE), snaptitude/AS; 1, Mtsaride/SS; 2 (field), TAlex/AS; 2, OSTILL is Franck Camhi/SS; 3, Mtsaride/SS; 4-5, Eugene Onischenko/SS; 6, Allen Kee/ESPN Images; 7, Scott Clarke/ESPN Images; 8 (BACKGROUND), koson_thamai/AS; 8, OSTILL/GI; 10 (LE), Francis Miller/The LIFE Picture Collection/SS (12049271a); 10 (LO), MediaNews Group/Reading Eagle/GI; 11 (UP), Underwood Archives/GI; 11 (LO), Jeff Vinnick/GI; 12 (UP), Wilfredo Lee/photographer; 12 (CTR), AP Photo/Stew Milne; 12 (LO), Jamie Squire/GI; 13 (UP), Scott Halleran/GI; 13 (CTR), Bettmann/GI; 13 (LO RT), Jamie Squire/GI; 13 (LO CTR), Neil Leifer /Sports Illustrated via GI; 14, Allan Dranberg/CSM/SS; 15 (UP), AP Photo/Wade Payne; 15 (LO), Icon Sportswire/GI; 16 (UP), AP Photo/Adrian Kraus; 16 (LO), AP Photo/Sue Ogrocki; 17 (UP), cmannphoto/GI; 17 (LO), Kevin C. Cox/GI; 18, Chris Graythen/GI; 19, Icon Sportswire/GI; 20 (UP), Brian Blanco/GI; 20 (LO), Krivosheev Vitaly/SS; 21 (LE), dean bertoncelj/SS; 21 (RT), Joe Sargent/GI; 22, Pete Saloutos/SS; 23, Heritage Auctions, Dallas; 24, Alesandro14/SS; 25, Robert Arthur Designs/SS; 25 (CTR), Collegiate Images/GI; 25 (LO), Danny E Hooks/SS; 26 (UP), Ken Durden/SS; 26 (LO), Brent Just/GI; 27 (UP), Library of Congress Prints and Photographs Division; 27 (LO), Icon Sportswire/GI; 28 (UP), Icon Sportswire/GI; 28 (LO), Kevork Djansezian/GI; 29, Greg Nelson/GI; 30 (UP), Icon Sportswire/GI; 30 (LE), Jason Miller/GI; 30 (LO), Doug Pensinger/GI; 31 (UP), Abbie Parr/GI; 31 (CTR RT), Boston Globe/GI; 31 (LO RT), Julio Aguilar/GI; 31 (CTR LE), Doug Benc/GI; 31 (LO LE), Scott Taetsch/GI; 32 (LE), Elnur/GI; 32 (RT), BillionPhotos/AS; 33 (UP), Donald Miralle/GI; 33 (UP RT), Hill Street Studios/GI; 33 (LO), Hyoung Chang/GI; 34 (UP), Eliot J. Schechter/GI; 34 (LO), slobo/GI; 35 (UP), Icon Sportswire/GI; 35 (CTR), Bloomberg/GI; 35 (LO), Elsa/GI; 36 (CTR), Christine Kohler/GI; 36 (LO RT), razihusin/AS; 36 (LO LE), ejwhite/GI; 37, ti-ja/GI; 38, OSTILL is Franck Camhi/SS; 40 (UP), AP Photo/Joe Robbins; 40 (LO), Jamie Squire/GI; 40 (LE), Jamie Sabau/GI; 41 (UP), Jonathan Bachman/GI; 41 (LO), Brocreative/SS; 42 (UP), Icon Sportswire/GI; 42 (LO), John Weast/GI; 43 (UP), Doug Pensinger/GI; 43 (LO RT), Gregory Shamus/GI; 43 (LO LE), AP Photo/Nick Wass; 44, Rob Tringali/Sportschrome/GI; 45 (UP), New York Daily News/GI; 45 (CTR), GI; 45 (LO), AP Photo/RGB; 46 (UP), AP Photo/Frank Gunn; 46 (LE), Focus On Sport/GI; 46-47 (LO), Focus On Sport/GI; 47 (UP), Focus On Sport/GI; 47 (CTR), Focus On Sport/GI; 47 (LO RT), Bettmann/GI; 48-49, Alesandro14/SS; 50 (UP RT), James Flores/GI; 50 (UP LE), Rhona Wise/GI; 50 (LO), Maddie Meyer/GI; 51, AP Photo; 52, Bettmann/GI; 53 (UP), AP Photo/Robert Walsh; 53 (LO), Vic Stein/GI; 54 (UP), XFL/GI; 54 (LO), Icon Sportswire/GI; 56 (UP), Sports Illustrated/GI; 56 (CTR), GI; 56 (LO), Pro Football Hall of Fame via AP; 57 (UP), Ron Vesely/GI; 57 (LO RT), Scott Grant; 57 (LO LE), Fred Roe/GI; 57 (CTR LE), Focus On Sport/GI; 58 (UP), VitaminCo/SS; 58 (CTR), Lane Oatey/GI; 58 (LO), tammykay-photo/SS; 60, Dmytro Aksonov/GI; 62, Joe Robbins/GI; 63, Adam Glanzman/GI; 64 (UP), AP Photo; 64 (LO), Bettmann/GI; 65, Paul Buck/GI; 65 (LO), Rick Stewart/GI; 66, Icon Sportswire/GI; 67 (RT), Joe Scarnici/GI; 67 (LO), Icon Sportswire/GI; 68 (UP), Brad Mangin/GI; 68 (CTR), Stephen Dunn/GI; 68 (LO), Andy Hayt/GI; 69 (UP), Tony Tomsic/GI; 69 (CTR), Tony Tomsic/GI; 69 (LO), Heritage Images/GI; 70 (UP), Elsa/GI; 70 (CTR), Owen C. Shaw/GI; 70 (LO), Robert B. Stanton/GI; 71 (UP), Bettmann/GI; 71 (LO), Jeff Kowalsky/GI; 72 (UP), aneduard/AS; 72 (CTR LE), Double Brain/SS; 72 (CTR), PrimaStockPhoto/SS; 72 (CTR RT), Fotokostic/SS; 73, SOPA Images/GI; 73 (LO), Pamela Uyttendaele/SS; 74, Collegiate Images/GI; 75 (Bears), Icon Sportswire/GI; 75 (Steelers), Jeff Bukowski/SS; 75 (Packers), Jeff Bukowski/SS; 76 (UP), Jacob Kupferman/GI; 76 (LO), Focus On Sport/GI; 77 (UP), AP Photo/G. Newman Lowrance; 77 (LO), Allen Kee/GI; 79, Jeff Haynes/GI; 80 (UP), Focus On Sport/GI; 80 (LO RT), Focus On Sport/GI; 80 (LO LE), Focus On Sport/GI; 81 (UP), Focus On Sport/GI; 81 (CTR LE), Tony Tomsic/GI; 81 (LO RT), Bettmann/GI; 82 (UP), AP Photo/Jack Smith; 82 (LO RT), Fred Ross/GI; 82 (LO LE), Tony Tomsic/GI; 83 (UP), Focus On Sport/GI; 83 (CTR), Neil Leifer/GI; 83 (LO), Jeff Haynes/GI; 84 (UP), noraismail/SS; 84 (LO), JoeSAPhotos/SS; 85, filo/GI; 86 (UP), NurPhoto/GI; 86 (LO), Minas Panagiotakis/GI; 87 (LE), Jerome Davis/GI; 87 (RT), Christian Petersen/GI; 87 (LE), Jerome Davis/GI; 87 (RT), Christian Petersen/GI; 88 (UP), Andre Ringuette/Freestyle Photo/GI; 88 (CTR), Rey Del Rio/GI; 88 (LO), AP Photo/David Durochik; 89 (UP), Collegiate Images/GI; 89 (LO), Christian Petersen/GI; 90 (UP), enterlinedesign/SS; 90 (LO RT), Brocreative/SS; 90 (LO LE), Air Images/SS; 91 (UP), nullplus/GI; 91 (LO), 33ft/GI; 92, OSTILL is Franck Camhi/SS; 94, Focus On Sport/GI; 95 (UP), Bloomberg/GI; 95 (LO), Deanne Fitzmaurice/GI; 96 (UP), Robert Riger/GI; 96 (LO), Rob Carr/GI; 97 (UP), Joseph Patronite/GI; 97 (CTR), Al Bello/GI; 97 (LO), avs/SS; 98, Tom Pennington/GI; 100 (UP), Hulton Archive/GI; 100 (LO), Kevork Djansezian/GI; 101 (UP), Sean Gardner/GI; 101 (CTR), Joel Auerbach/GI; 101 (LO), Stephen Dunn/GI; 102 (UP), C. Morgan Engel/GI; 102 (LO), Kevin C. Cox/GI; 103 (UP), Jamie Schwaberow/GI; 103 (LO), Ronald Martinez/GI; 104, Brent Just/GI; 105 (UP), Andre Ringuette/GI; 105 (CTR), Andre Ringuette/GI; 105 (LO), John E. Sokolowski/GI; 106 (UP), Mike Ehrmann/GI; 106 (LO), Chris Graythen/GI; 107 (UP), Ezra Shaw/GI; 107 (CTR), Maddie Meyer/GI; 107 (LO), Katelyn Mulcahy/GI; 108 (UP), rangizzz/SS; 108 (LO), Artem Varnitsin/EyeEm/GI; 109, mixetto/GI; 110, OSTILL is Franck Camhi/SS; 112 (UP), Georgetown University Archives; 112 (LO), George Gojkovich/GI; 113 (ALL), Georgia Tech Archives; 114 (ALL), John Biever/GI; 115 (UP), Bettmann/GI; 115 (LO RT), John Mahler/GI; 115 (LO LE), Library and Archives Canada; 116 (UP), Neil Leifer/GI; 116 (LO), Andre Ringuette/GI; 117 (UP), Hunter Martin/GI; 117 (CTR), Sam Greenwood/GI; 117 (LO), Ezra Shaw/GI; 118, George Long/GI; 119 (UP), Justin Casterline/GI; 119 (LO), Tim Umphrey/GI; 120, Donald Miralle/GI; 121, Mike Powell/GI; 122, AP Photo/Pro Football Hall of Fame; 123 (UP), B Bennett/GI; 123 (CTR), Gregory Shamus/GI; 123 (LO RT), Jonathan Bachman/GI; 123 (LO LE), Diamond Images/GI

INDEX

MATH TEACHER REFERENCE

Since 1888, the National Geographic Society has funded more than 14,000 research, conservation, education, and storytelling projects around the world. National Geographic Partners distributes a portion of the funds it receives from your purchase to National Geographic Society to support programs including the conservation of animals and their habitats. To learn more, visit natgeo.com/info.

For more information, visit nationalgeographic.com, call 1-877-873-6846, or write to the following address:

National Geographic Partners, LLC
1145 17th Street NW
Washington, DC 20036-4688 U.S.A.

For librarians and teachers: nationalgeographic.com/books/librarians-and-educators

More for kids from National Geographic: natgeokids.com

National Geographic Kids magazine inspires children to explore their world with fun yet educational articles on animals, science, nature, and more. Using fresh storytelling and amazing photography, *Nat Geo Kids* shows kids ages 6 to 14 the fascinating truth about the world—and why they should care. **natgeo.com/subscribe**

For rights or permissions inquiries, please contact National Geographic Books Subsidiary Rights: bookrights@natgeo.com

Thank you to Kim Adams, Erica Alexander, Bob Colgate, Margie McGill, Lyle McKellar, Pat Park, and Tracy Sturgeon. Also to the men and women who compile the rule books and record books for the CFL, NFL, and NCAA, the guide book to the Pro Football Hall of Fame, and the website of the Canadian Football Hall of Fame. The publisher would like to thank the following for making this book come together: Angela Modany, editor; Erica J. Green, project editor; Julide Dengel, senior designer; Sarah J. Mock, senior photo editor; Matt Propert, photo editor; Eva Absher, director, art and design; Gail Burrill, expert reviewer; Jim Reid, expert reviewer; Robin Palmer, fact checker; Rachel Ullrich, ESPN deputy editor; Molly Reid, production editor; and Gus Tello and Anne LeongSon, associate designers.

Library of Congress Cataloging-in-Publication Data

Names: Zweig, Eric, 1963- author.
Title: It's a numbers game : football / Eric Zweig.
Description: Washington, D.C. : National Geographic Partners, LLC, 2022. I Includes index. I Audience: Ages 8-12 I Audience: Grades 4-6
Identifiers: LCCN 2021011561 I ISBN 9781426372896 (hardcover) I ISBN 9781426372902 (library binding)
Subjects: LCSH: Football--Statistical methods--Juvenile literature. I Football--Mathematical models--Juvenile literature.
Classification: LCC GV950.7 .Z94 2022 I DDC 796.332--dc23
LC record available at https://lccn.loc.gov/2021011561

Printed in China
23/PPS/2

To Lynn. Thanks for putting up with me during the FFB and for your love and support in so many ways.

—Eric Zweig

EXPERT REVIEWERS

Jim Reid has coached NCAA and NFL football for a total of 48 years, with stints as head coach at the University of Massachusetts Amherst and the University of Richmond, defensive coordinator at Boston College and the University of Virginia, and linebackers coach for the Miami Dolphins and the University of Iowa Hawkeyes. His career includes multiple coach of the year honors at the University of Massachusetts Amherst and University of Richmond and appearances in NFL playoffs as well as major bowls, including the Rose Bowl, Peach Bowl, Fiesta Bowl, Outback Bowl, and Pinstripe Bowl.

Gail Burrill, now in the Program in Mathematics Education at Michigan State University, was a secondary mathematics teacher for over 28 years. She received the Presidential Award for Excellence in Teaching Mathematics, is a T3 National Instructor and elected member of the International Statistics Institute, and served as President of the National Council of Teachers of Mathematics and as President of the International Association of Statistical Education.